The
STOIC
ART *of*
LIVING

The STOIC ART *of* LIVING

Inner Resilience and Outer Results

TOM MORRIS

Author of *The Art of Achievement* and *Philosophy for Dummies*

OPEN COURT
Chicago and La Salle, Illinois

To order books from Open Court, call toll-free 1-800-815-2280, or visit our website at www.opencourtbooks.com.

Open Court Publishing Company is a division of Carus Publishing Company.

Printed and bound in the United States of America.

Library of Congress Cataloging-in-Publication Data

Morris, Thomas V.
    The stoic art of living : inner resilience and outer results / Tom Morris.
        p.   cm.
    Includes index.
    ISBN 0-8126-9570-4 (alk. paper)—ISBN 0-8126-9559-3 (pbk. : alk. paper)
    1. Stoics. 2. Conduct of life.   I. Title.
    B528.M675 2004
    188—dc22

                                                                    2004004038

CONTENTS

PART III
Wise Words on Life Straight from the Top
The Imperial Insights of Marcus Aurelius   119

ACKNOWLEDGMENTS

I've enjoyed reading the Stoics for years and writing up short essays on how their thoughts apply to our lives in the modern world. Some of these essays have been mailed out to corporate executives whose companies I've served as a philosopher, and others have been posted on my website, www.MorrisInstitute.com. I want to thank all those friends and website visitors who've given me their personal and professional comments on these essays over the years. I encourage all readers of this little book to visit my outpost in cyberspace for more philosophical interaction at any time.

Once again, I want to thank my wife and children—Mary, Sara, and Matt—for their encouragement and goodwill in this and all my projects. Having them as my support network, along with Bailey, Daisy, and Lexie—three great dogs—has kept my life balanced and fun.

I'd like to dedicate this book to all my friends at the Washington Speakers Bureau who help me bring the wisdom of the great thinkers into the lives of people who can use it now.

INTRODUCTION

If you live long enough and pay attention to what you see, you may come to understand one of the deepest truths about life: Inner resilience is the secret to outer results in this world. Challenging times demand inner strength and a spirit that won't be defeated. And, as a philosopher, I've come to understand that nearly all the times we live in are in some sense challenging.

When things are really bad, it's hard to keep your faith. When things are very good, it's tough to keep your head. In tragedy, it's difficult to be hopeful. In triumph, it's hard to be humble. In either case, maintaining a proper perspective on life is the challenge. And in those occasionally long stretches of time when things seem not to be either great or terrible, it's often tough to remember and prepare for the amazing extremes that life can hold.

The wisdom of perspective is perhaps one of the most difficult things to achieve and maintain throughout the vicissitudes we inevitably experience in this world. Our lives can sometimes feel like a wild roller-coaster ride. A long climb of hopeful striving may culminate in an exhilarating high, and then the bottom falls out and we find ourselves suddenly plunging into a dark abyss, scared and apparently out of control.

How can we keep our balance when life threatens to throw us completely? How can we make the most of our talents and energies in such an unpredictable world? Is any form of enduring success and personal happiness even possible when, on any given day, it can feel like we're running through a minefield and dodging potential disaster with every step?

A group of ancient philosophers known as the Stoics had some powerful answers to these questions. Three thinkers in particular, living during the Golden Age of Rome, saw that the strength of inner resilience is the secret to personal effectiveness; that inner peace is, for most of us, the missing link to personal happiness; and that a nobility of self-possession and emotional self-control can make all the difference for living a life in full command of its own resources, and with a deep enjoyment of its intrinsic rewards. The Stoics saw what we need. And they left us some powerful advice about how to find it in our lives.

It's truly astonishing to see the penetrating relevance today of wisdom articulated by a few thinkers who grappled with life in a very different time and place, the first and second century Roman world. But human nature never really changes. And the insights we need never really vary. It's the soul that's more important than the body, the inner that's more important than the outer, and our character that's the ultimate source of true success and personal fulfillment. We need to learn what we do have control over in life and recognize what too often has control over us. We need to concentrate on what really matters, free ourselves from a deep philosophical slavery to false schemes of life, and focus on doing the good we can for others as well as ourselves. These simple but powerful Stoic themes are capable of changing our lives. They can point us in the direction of worthwhile achievement, and put within our reach the genuine personal happiness that comes only from a life fully and properly lived.

THE PRACTICAL ADVICE OF THE STOICS

The most popular and influential Stoic philosophers were practical thinkers. Epictetus was a slave. Seneca was a lawyer. Marcus Aurelius was Emperor of Rome. From the bottom of society, to the upwardly mobile middle, and all the way to the top, these three ancient thinkers saw life deeply. And they can provide us with great advice on how to live it.

Epictetus, like Socrates long before him, did not write. He talked to people eager to understand life. And one of his students took down his words of wisdom. Unlike Epictetus, Seneca wrote volumes. But much of his greatest wisdom is contained in personal letters and short essays he composed for the instruction and inspiration of friends. Marcus Aurelius kept a notebook of thoughts about life for his own use. None of these great Stoics wrote self-help or personal growth books for broad audiences of contemporary readers, but from what they did say or write, from their very different and yet deeply similar life experiences, we can glean tremendous insight for how to live noble and creative lives now.

In this little book, my aim is to present their best nuggets of wisdom on topics that are of pressing interest to most of us these days. What does it take to live successfully in such a tumultuous world? What is the role of character, and virtue, in business achievement, and personal happiness? How should we deal with the difficulties and sufferings we inevitably face in life, and how can we prevail?

This is not an academic or scholarly study, and it doesn't purport to give a comprehensive or thematically representative look at Stoic philosophy, its origins, influences, or development through the centuries. I'm just mining a rich vein of advice in the best of Stoic wisdom that can be applied to our lives now. There is no big-scale political philosophy here. There are no attempts to answer all the cosmic questions. In response to our deep current need for the most practical advice of the Stoics, I've brought together a pointed and useful collection of their insights, showing how they fit together into a pattern of powerful recommendations for good living.

These Stoics did not think in a vacuum. They were influenced by the work of many other philosophers. But each of them engaged first hand in trying to understand life. And, by their example, we can all see how to do it for ourselves. At its best, philosophy is an activity to be pursued by every thoughtful person. It's not an enterprise of purely esoteric speculation reserved for ancient minds with nothing better to do. It's not a dusty museum of past masters. Philosophy is a vibrant quest to know, to understand, and finally, to act—with wisdom.

WISDOM FOR LIVING

In one of his letters, Seneca defined the enterprise of philosophy quite simply. He wrote:

> Wisdom is the perfect good of the human mind;
> Philosophy is the love of wisdom, and the endeavor
> to attain it.

Explaining why he thinks of wisdom in such high terms, in another passage, he calls it simply "the art of living." He then summarizes the task of philosophy like this:

> Would you really like to know what philosophy
> offers humanity? Philosophy offers counsel.

It is some of that counsel, that wise advice for living, that we're going to consult, and draw insight from, in these pages.

For Seneca, going to the words and wisdom of the philosophers of the past is an imminently practical act. It's never just for intellectual enlightenment, but always for help in living well. He writes:

> Unless we are very ungrateful, all these men, these
> glorious creators of holy thoughts, were born for us.
> They have prepared for us a way of life.

This philosopher believed that if we approach with the right attitude the writings that other good thinkers have left us, we'll always learn and grow:

> He who studies with a philosopher should take
> away one good thing each day: He should return
> home a healthier man, or at least on the way to
> becoming healthier.

Philosophy gives us good advice. It can light our paths and change our lives. We can indeed become sounder, stronger, and happier people by applying its wisdom.

OUR PATHS THROUGH LIFE

There are some deep similarities in the perspectives of two of our three thinkers I should note in advance. In reading Seneca, the accomplished and politically well-placed lawyer, and in meditating on Emperor Marcus Aurelius's reflections on life, I have seen a pattern of advice having to do with the living of a successful life that is interestingly consistent with the writings of other great thinkers from diverse cultures and different historical periods. Their individual perspectives are distinctive, and specific Stoic themes always come through, but these two counselors of the soul reinforce some major insights discerned by many other philosophers in very different traditions as well, both east and west. To me, this just testifies to the universality of their wisdom, and the universal grip of their principles for successful living.

Seneca and Marcus Aurelius will make clear that our life goals need to be rooted in self-knowledge, must be guided by a sense of what is good, and should take form within an ennobling big picture for all our efforts. They will offer sound advice for steering our actions through days of difficulty and times of joy. As the most socially accomplished of the popular Stoic philosophers, it will be predominantly their thoughts on proper success along life's journey that we'll be drawing on in what follows.

Epictetus is a different bird altogether. While sharing so many of the basic perspectives of his fellow Stoic thinkers, he saw life from a distinctive vantage point. Having lived as a slave, and subsequently as a free teacher of philosophy, and then having been banished by Emperor Domitian, along with all other philosophers, in A.D. 89, he moved to the beach to share his wisdom with anyone who cared to visit. He lived simply and thought hard about the surprising difficulties we often face in life. It's his perspectives on freedom, character, inner strength and the power of attitude that we'll explore most. Epictetus realized that, despite what the world around us often tries to tell us, very little is needed for a good life. But what is needed is inner and is vital. And it's that vital inner essence of the truly good life that we'll explore in these pages.

In what follows, I'll be drawing on various source materials, in consultation with the work of many other translators, and I'll be offering my own renderings of the meaning I see in the original Greek and Latin. For the convenience of the reader, my source references throughout the text will be to the following: *The Loeb Classical Library Volumes of Seneca,* Harvard University Press: *Epistulae Morales (EM) I, II,* and *III* (translated by Richard Gummere), *Moral Essays (ME) I* and *II* (translated by J.W. Basore), and *Epistles 66–99* (translated by Richard Gummere); *The Loeb Classical Library Volumes of Epictetus,* Harvard University Press: *Discourses, Books I–II,* and *Discourses, Books III–IV, with The Encheiridion* (translated by W.A. Oldfather); as well as to *The Loeb Classical Library Marcus Aurelius,* Harvard University Press, (edited and translated by C.R. Haines). In my references, I use abbreviations when there are multiple sources. For Epictetus, numerals alone refer to the *Discourses*, 'E' references the *Encheiridion*, and 'F' refers to *The Fragments*, as numbered in *The Discourses of Epictetus, With the Encheiridion and Fragments*, A.L. Burt Company (translated by George Long). For further reading, you may want to see *The Stoic Philosophy of Seneca*, Norton (translated by Moses Hadas) and *The Meditations of Marcus Aurelius*, Avon Books, 1993 (translated by George Long), as well as some nice recent translations of the *Meditations*: the Modern Library Edition, 2002 (translated by Gregory Hays), and *The Emperor's Handbook*, Scribner, 2002 (translated by C. Scott Hicks and David V. Hicks).

PART I

A LAWYER'S ADVICE FOR LIFE IN THE FAST LANE

The Wisdom of Seneca

A COUNSELOR IN THE
COURT OF LIFE

The Stoic philosopher Seneca lived in the fast lane of the first century for a long time before he was forced down the off-ramp. And he left us lots of great advice on how not to crash and burn as we pursue our own high-speed dreams along the road of life.

Lucius Annaeus Seneca (around 4 B.C.–A.D. 65) was an extraordinarily insightful lawyer, senator, philosopher, and playwright of the first century. He was born in Spain, but early on moved to Rome, where he was educated and became involved in affairs of state. This influential Stoic writer and powerful public speaker inflamed jealousy in the emperor Caligula and barely escaped being murdered by him. He later tutored the young Nero and, early on, helped keep in check some of the young man's more unfortunate behavioral tendencies.

Seneca is sometimes criticized for allegedly not living up to his own high moral standards, because he lived and grew very wealthy at a court where his announced moral principles were basically repudiated. But on examination, the charge seems unfair. It's undeniable that Seneca did have a restraining moral influence on many of those around him. When Nero's conduct deteriorated dramatically, the philosopher withdrew from public and political life, and even offered to return his wealth to the emperor. Later ordered to commit suicide, he passed the ultimate test of behaving consistently with his own philosophical view that the end of life is not to be feared, and, like Socrates before him, complied.

Seneca thought of himself first and foremost as a philosopher. He invested great energy in reflecting on life and how to live it well. In his letters and essays, we often come across pithy wisdom that can help us rethink our own perspectives on life. For example, in an essay reflecting on the brevity of our existence on earth, he writes:

CHAPTER 1

> The problem is not that we have such a short
> space of time, but that we waste so much of it. Life
> is long enough, and it has been given in sufficiently
> generous measure, to allow the accomplishment of
> the very greatest things if the whole of it is well
> invested. (ME II, 289)

This investment counselor of the soul wrote his many letters and essays to help his friends, and posterity, make the most of what this life has to offer. He wanted to help us avoid wasting our days on trivial pursuits and guide us to seek the most important things in life instead.

To this end, Seneca recommended from deep personal experience that we should continue to develop our minds throughout life, long after our formal educations have concluded, by exercising our intellects on an ongoing basis, primarily with the help of philosophy. As our philosopher puts it:

> The mind should be exercised both day and night
> because it is nourished by moderate labor. And this
> form of exercise need not be hampered by cold or
> hot weather, or even by old age. (EM I, 99)

It was his fervent belief that the enterprise of philosophy consists of:

> . . . those studies that best exalt prosperity and
> diminish adversity, and that are simultaneously both
> the greatest adornments and the greatest comforts
> for human beings. (ME II, 409–411)

According to Seneca, philosophy at its best is just the deepest possible study in the art of living.

Commenting on the nature of this distinctive activity that he was recommending to us all, Seneca specifies further that:

> Philosophy is no trick to catch the public—it's not
> devised for show. It deals with facts and not just
> words. It shouldn't be pursued so that the day may
> yield some amusement before it's over, or to keep us
> from being bored when we're not at work. It molds

and constructs the soul. It orders our lives. It
guides our conduct by showing us what we should
do and what we should leave undone. It sits at
the helm and directs our course when we waver
amid uncertainties. Without it, no one can live
fearlessly or with peace of mind. Countless things
that happen every day call for advice, and such
advice is to be sought in philosophy. (EM I, 105)

And, as if to put an exclamation point to the powers of philosophy
in human life, he claims, quite dramatically that:

Philosophy did not find Plato already a nobleman,
it made him one. (EM I, 289)

It was Seneca's unshakable conviction that philosophy of the right
sort can do the same for you and me.

2

THE PHILOSOPHER'S ADVICE

What exactly is this enterprise of philosophy that a practical man of the world like Seneca is praising and recommending so highly? What can it do for us? Philosophy, in the hands of a thinker like Seneca, is an eminently practical enterprise. It has theoretical underpinnings, to be sure, but its ultimate goal is to inspire us to proper achievement and good living. The philosopher is a physician of the soul, whose advice aims at spiritual health and happiness.

Like physics, philosophy seeks to understand the most ultimate realities with which we have to do. Yet, unlike physics, the philosophy most true to human nature gives us not technical terminology and news of marvels outside the ken of our normal experience, but rather reminders of what lies right in front of our eyes, or, if we are perceptive, inside our own hearts.

It has even sometimes been said that philosophy, at its best, is just "common sense in dress clothes." In ancient Greece, the famous Socrates had often described himself as a midwife of the mind, merely helping people give birth to thoughts that were already deep within them. In the philosophical advice Seneca gives us about successful living, we often find ourselves experiencing a clear and dramatic statement of what we have always somehow suspected or even in some sense known. But, then, this easily could be thought to create a problem. What's the point of telling us things we already know?

Our advisor has a great answer:

> People say: "What good does it do to point out the obvious?" A great deal of good, since we sometimes know facts without paying attention to them.

> Advice is not the same thing as teaching. It just
> gets our attention and wakes us up, and concentrates
> our memory and keeps it from losing its grip. We
> otherwise miss a lot that's right in front of our eyes.
> Advice is, in fact, a sort of exhortation. (EM III, 29)

In one of the best books written by an individual highly successful in the world of sports, *Sacred Hoops*, the Los Angeles Lakers, and former Chicago Bulls, championship basketball coach Phil Jackson draws on the insights of philosophy and emphasizes more than once the central importance of focused mental attention in everything we do. The world's great religious traditions have always stressed the importance of what commands our attention. So it's no surprise to see a perceptive thinker like Seneca speak here of attention as crucially important to the impact of philosophy. Philosophy at its best, he says, focuses our attention on things that might have eluded us because of their very familiarity, reminds us of important truths that we need to act on, and then goads us into action as well. He continues by saying,

> Whatever is good for us should be discussed often
> and frequently brought to mind, so that it may
> be not just familiar to us, but also ready for use.
> Remember also that in this way what is clear often
> becomes clearer. (EM III, 29)

Seneca developed wisdom about prosperity and successful living that resonates with some of the best contemporary thought concerning happiness and the good life. His nuggets of advice often help us to understand more thoroughly any insights we might already have managed to grasp about true success in life. What is clear becomes clearer, and deep realizations that might have remained unarticulated are suddenly sparked into consciousness as we read his words. He provides us with elements of a life guidance tool kit that display a logical unity, a form of inner coherence, and a tremendous usefulness for anyone living in tumultuous times.

The philosopher himself reflects on the overall role of good advice and says:

> The soul carries within itself the seed of everything
> that is honorable, and this seed is stirred to growth

> by advice, as a spark fanned by a gentle breeze
> develops its natural fire. Virtue is aroused by a
> touch, or a shock. In addition, there are certain
> things that, although they are already in our
> minds, are not all ready for use, but begin to
> function easily as soon as they're put into words.
> Some things lie scattered around in various places,
> and it is impossible for the unpracticed mind to
> arrange them in a proper order. We need to bring
> them into unity and join them, so that they can be
> more powerful and more of an uplift to the soul.
> (EM III, 31)

The human mind is often like a large cluttered closet, packed full of good stuff but so messy and disorganized we can easily forget what we've got in there. And, of course, you can't use what you can't find, or don't even remember you have. For most of us, the task of organizing all that stuff is just too daunting to attempt. A philosopher like Seneca is something of a master organizer, with ideas that can help us to recognize, access, organize and use all that we've learned about life so far. He can help us make the most of the wisdom we already have, and in the process give us room to acquire more.

The power of Seneca's advice lies not just in its universality of application, but in its ability to spark us and fan us into flaming action, guiding that action from within our own hearts, and moving us out into the world. It can help bring into powerful unity the various insights and habits for successful living that we already have picked up along the way, and it can give us fresh perspectives on what it takes for satisfying, sustainable achievement in our world. Seneca himself would certainly remind us that it is not just the nuggets of wisdom themselves, but how we apply them, that is the ultimate aim of philosophy. The proper application of any insight, however, depends on the proper perspective. Seneca always wants to give us his advice not just with regard to the details of our lives, but within the setting of the bigger picture of life that philosophy, at its best, always presents. He maintains:

> It is not enough, when a man is arranging his
> existence as a whole, just to give him advice on the
> details. (EM III, 87)

Seneca can help us with the big picture, as well as with the particulars. He comes to us not as a psychologist with context-relative tips and techniques, but as a philosopher with deep truths to orient our own journeys through life so that we can attain the right sort of success along the way. He wants to help us find an overall philosophy to inspire us and guide us into the virtue, or strength, that we need for the challenging adventure we're all on in this world. And he reminds us that we must both learn it and live it if we are to benefit deeply from it:

> Virtue depends partly on training and partly on practice. You must learn first, and then strengthen what you've learned by practice. (EM III, 41)

Our philosopher realizes that the advice he gives won't always be easy to put into practice, but he assures us that he has real people like us in mind when he gives it. Seneca insists:

> I need to remind you, over and over, that I am
> not speaking about an ideal wise man to whom
> every duty is a pleasure, and who rules over
> his own spirit, imposing on himself any law he
> pleases, while always obeying what he has imposed,
> but I am talking about anyone who, with all his
> imperfections, desires to follow the perfect path,
> and yet has passions that often are reluctant to
> obey. (ME III, 87)

If we truly desire to live good and happy lives, we qualify as fit pupils for this philosopher. And with all the troubles we inevitably face in the world, we need this lawyer of life to help defend us against the many forces that would imprison us. If we listen well, and put into practice the best of his counsel, we can liberate ourselves to be our best and feel our best in all that we do.

CLARITY FOR THE
JOURNEY

Too many of us seem to stumble through life in a daze, or in a haze of vague expectations, and yet, oddly, that doesn't slow us down at all. The world seems to be full of people who are in a tremendous rush without knowing exactly where they are going. Capturing the nature of common human experience, Seneca points out:

> We don't recognize either what hurts us or what helps us. All through our lives we blunder along and never stop, or even watch our step, because of this. But surely you can see how crazy it is to rush ahead in the dark. We seem set on getting ourselves called back from a greater distance and, although we don't know our overall goal, we continue to move as fast as we can in the direction we're already going. (EM III, 269)

The consequences of failing to set clear life goals that are right for us, and instead just going with the flow, are not often very positive. We sometimes seem to be no more than passengers in a rudderless raft shooting down a fast moving river in directions that are not of our own choosing. Seneca says:

> It's disgraceful when, instead of steering your way forward, you find yourself carried along and suddenly, in a whirlpool of events, get so confused you ask: "How did I get into this condition?" (EM I, 257)

In archery, we aim at a target. In golf, we shoot for the pin. In sailing, we head for a port. Yet in life generally, we often neglect this sort of specific directedness, and suffer the consequences.

> The archer must know what he's trying to hit, then
> he must aim and control the weapon by his skill.
> Our plans miscarry because they have no aim. When
> a man does not know what harbor he is heading
> for, no wind is the right wind. (Ep. 75)

In recent years, many business consultants and life advisors have insisted that, in every endeavor, we always "Begin with the end in view." Seneca puts it like this:

> Let all your effort be directed toward some object,
> let it always keep some goal in view! (ME II, 265)

If we know where we're going, we're in the best position to make the most of the things that come our way. Philosophers have long seen that opportunity surrounds us constantly, but if we are not ordering our minds and efforts around goals that structure our perceptions and intentions, we will not be in the right frame of mind to perceive those opportunities as they arise, to appreciate them as such, and to make the most of them for our own good as well as for the good of the people around us. Seneca believes in goal setting as a crucial first step in any quest of achievement, and as an ongoing exercise necessary for any successful journey.

But just as important as goal setting is proper goal setting. People too often chase the wrong things. If we are pursuing inappropriate goals, we guarantee our own dissatisfaction. When our goals are wrong for us, achieving them will not satisfy us, and failing to attain them will disappoint us unnecessarily. But then, the question is: How can we see to it that we are setting the right goals for ourselves daily, weekly, monthly, and through the years? Seneca suggests that we need to orient all our goals within the broader horizons of an overarching purpose. He says:

> The reason we make mistakes is because we all
> consider the parts of life, but never life as a whole.
> (Ep. 73)

It is life as a whole that philosophy, at its best, helps us to grasp.

If we don't understand human nature, we won't set ourselves the best goals. A vast army of motivational speakers for decades have promised their audiences that, "You can get anything you want as long as you help enough other people get what they want." To my knowledge, this claim was first made in recent times by Zig Ziglar, an enthusiastic public speaker who seeks to espouse in his talks a wise and properly ethical perspective on personal success. But the philosophical concern that someone like Seneca would have concerning this specific claim and the way it is worded can be raised by wondering whether what we happen to want at any given time would be truly good for us, and whether playing to what other people also happen to want is itself always a good thing.

On the one hand, it does seem to signal an ethical point of view to put other people's wants prior to your own, and to work at satisfying their desires, trusting that, as a result, yours will then more likely be taken care of as well. But what if those other people want something that is not truly good for them, something that would even diminish them as human beings? A film producer who gets rich making gory exploitation movies might preach to a colleague his own philosophy of blatant manipulation by saying that, "You can get anything you want if you help enough other people get what they want." So, what's being left out here?

In charting our course through life, we need to consider not just what it is that we and others do want, but what we should want, what would be genuinely good for us as human beings. Seneca says that we should derive our ultimate orientation in goal setting by asking what is supremely good, and pursuing that in all we do:

> We should clearly envision as our goal the Supreme Good, as something toward which we can work, and to which all our actions and words can be directed—just as sailors must guide their course by a certain star. Life without ideals is erratic. And as soon as an ideal is set up, doctrines begin to be necessary. (EM III, 87)

Desires and wants are fine, but ideals are even more important for the enterprise of proper goal setting. Our desires do not always guide us well. We need a conception of what is supremely good for human life, we need some ideals, and we need something else that is often translated here, a bit awkwardly, as "doctrines". The Latin word is *decreta*, a plural term often translated as "decrees". But that word itself is derived from the preposition *de*, meaning "from," and the verb *cernere*, meaning "to discern", "to perceive", or "to distinguish. " I think Seneca is saying here not that we need "doctrines," a word with all sorts of institutional and dogmatic connotations, but that when we have properly high ideals, we need some moral principles based on those things that we perceive to be absolutely good—clear and specific principles that will help us draw distinctions between what is worthy and what is not, and thus give us guidelines to distinguish what we should pursue from what we most properly should just leave alone.

Our philosopher elsewhere elaborates:

> Whenever you want to know what should be avoided
> or what should be pursued, consider its relation to
> the Supreme Good, to the purpose of your entire life.
> Whatever we do ought to be in harmony with this
> truth: no one can set in order the details unless he
> has first set in his mind the chief purpose of his life.
> (Ep, 73)

We most often allow ourselves to be launched into our adult lives and into our careers without enough guidance from the realm of what really matters. Our educations are too often no more than technical training in the how-to of human activity with scant attention to the whys and deeper what-for of life. Seneca writes:

> The soul should know where it is going and where
> it has been, what is good for it and what is evil,
> what it seeks and what it avoids, and what is the
> Reason that distinguishes between the desirable and
> the undesirable, and in that way tames the madness
> of our desires, and calms the violence of our fears.
> (Ep, 243–45)

This, of course, is a tall order. What is the purpose of your life? Where did you come from? Where are you going? What is genuinely good for you? What is evil? How can you best control self-destructive desires and overcome incapacitating fears? To some extent, the best answers to these questions are the result of living and thinking deeply. But Seneca believes we need some sense of these things as early as possible, to guide our paths through life at every point. Fortunately, we don't have to discover it all ourselves. We can turn to the philosophers who have gone before us and demonstrated how to deal with every one of these questions.

Some of the wisest people in history have suggested that the purpose of life is inner growth and outer service—developing and deepening your self, while working to help others do likewise. We are all called to provide for other people as well as ourselves what they and we most deeply need—the conditions for making the most of our journey. If you work to provide some measure of comfort, convenience, opportunity, education, or health for other people, you are helping to create the conditions under which their lives can be lived well. And the wonderful result is that, in serving others, you thereby are creating the conditions under which your own personal satisfaction and fulfillment is most likely to be attained. Such a sense of purpose then can guide your more specific goal setting and bring a solid dose of wisdom into your daily decisions. Those misguided individuals who selfishly seek only wealth, fame, power, or status for themselves and give little concern for others will never reliably set the sort of specific goals that are truly best for them to pursue. This is the message of the wisest philosophers.

When the soul knows itself, when we are thoroughly imbued with a conception of our own supreme good as human beings, then we are in a position for masterful and powerful goal setting. And in that position, Seneca recommends that we aim high. He declares:

> No man of exalted gifts is pleased with anything low and inferior. A vision of great achievement calls out to him and lifts him up. (EM I, 261)

The good news is that we all have important gifts, talents, and abilities. The trick is to develop them properly. Exalted goals rooted in our gifts ennoble us and inspire us to stretch and grow as people. Our overarching goals accordingly should always be high and noble ones that move in the right directions and embody what we see as the supreme good in our lives. Our smaller goals then should always fit consistently into those higher patterns of aspiration that are properly our long-term guides.

Aim high, Seneca urges, but be cautious at the same time. He advises:

> Whenever you want to attempt something, first measure both yourself and the task—the thing you intend and the thing for which you are intended. The regret that results from an unaccomplished task will make you bitter. (ME III, 271–73)

Know yourself. Get to know your proper purpose in life and in your career—"the thing for which you are intended"—and make sure you understand as well as possible the magnitude of any goal you consider embracing—take its measure as best you can before deciding to commit yourself. If we set inappropriate goals, or unreasonably difficult challenges at any given stage of our development, we run the risk of wasting our time and as a result undermining our own confidence in our abilities to pursue the goals that are important and right for us. Seneca counsels:

> Above all, it's necessary for anyone to judge himself accurately. We often think we can do more than we are able. (ME II, 235)

At a time when low levels of self-confidence seem rampant in the world, it can be odd to hear Seneca say that we ordinarily make the mistake of thinking we can do more than we actually are able to accomplish. But this is often exactly the mistake that especially ambitious people living in the fast lane are most apt to make. When they are offered an interesting opportunity, or hatch for themselves an exciting new plan, they very often tend to underestimate the amount of time and energy it will take to get the job done. Almost everything worth doing is harder than we think it should be. But that's O.K. as long as we come to understand this common gap between our expectations and reality.

Seneca continues to clarify his advice by saying:

> Next, we should weigh carefully what we are undertaking, and compare our strength with the things we are about to attempt. The doer should always be stronger than what he intends to do. Burdens too

heavy for their bearer will certainly crush him.
(ME II, 235)

The advice is basically simple. Know yourself, understand the task you're considering, and firmly grasp the relationship between its demands and your capacities. As very successful people know, an individual can be crushed by inordinate burdens in more than one way. A challenge can wear you out directly, or its pursuit can erode or obliterate some important aspect of your life, or even of your own spirit, if it is not right for you, in its shape and magnitude.

A task can crush us because it is too big, or because it takes us too far in a direction that is not right for us. Seneca says:

> Our next concern should be never to work either for useless goals, or impossible ones. First, we shouldn't even desire what we're completely unable to accomplish. And we ought not to seek anything that, if attained, will show us too late and after much shame the emptiness of our desires. In other words, our efforts should never be hopeless, and we shouldn't set goals unworthy of our work. Sadness will often follow a failure, and also the shame of an empty success. (ME II, 263)

He puts a part of his point quite succinctly like this:

> Some objects are superfluous, and others are not worth the price we pay for them. (EM I, 281)

This one insight can make the difference between happiness and misery, or satisfaction and disappointment, in anyone's life. I wish it could be printed on a greeting card and sent to everyone in America. Ophthalmologists and opticians should have it on their vision charts. It could do great good as a warning label on the face of every new credit card issued in the world. It might even serve well as the first, or perhaps the last, piece of advice any career counselor gives his advisees, or that parents pass on to their children, as they enter the world of work. Some things are just superfluous. Others aren't worth the price we have to pay for them.

Seneca then goes on to elaborate his insight in this way:

> All those things that delight us by their showy, but
> deceptive, charm—money, standing, power, and the
> many other things at the sight of which the human
> race, in its blind greed, is filled with awe—bring
> trouble to those who have them, stir jealousy in
> those who see them, and in the end crush the ones
> they adorn. They are more of a menace than a good.
> (ME II, 381)

We can be defeated in a futile attempt to attain a goal that is too challenging, or we can be crushed by the successful pursuit of a goal that is itself futile. Too many success books of the recent past show insufficient discrimination when it comes to the question of what we should pursue. They take it as their job just to help us get whatever we want. Seneca's point is that if we want and pursue the wrong things, our success will itself be burdensome and crushing.

Let me clarify quickly that Seneca had no intrinsic problem with money, fame or power. Throughout most of his life, he was wealthy, and was pleased to have ample resources. He was well known, and he wielded some measure of real social power. What he thought was inappropriate in human life is the avaricious pursuit of money, fame, power, and status as ends in themselves. Seneca believed that we are here in this world primarily to pursue wisdom and virtue, adornments of the inner self, not external things that can come or go at the bidding of forces beyond our control. Money can be a pleasant side effect of good work in the world, and so can a measure of recognition or power or status. But if these things are pursued as focal goals, the process of their achievement and the end state of their accomplishment can be equally crushing to the human spirit, which is intended to be geared primarily toward more inward and lasting realities.

We crave so much in the modern world. Advertising and the mass media present to us lustrous images of happy people delighted by their toys. And so we are tempted to chase the things we have thereby come to believe will satisfy us. But Seneca warns us that every single thing we gain by our work is purchased at a personal price. He therefore recommends:

> Let us therefore act, in all our plans and conduct,
> just as we do whenever we approach a huckster who
> has certain wares for sale. Let us see exactly how

much we'll have to pay for the things we crave.
(EM I, 283)

The goods of the external world are passing. So he counsels a different emphasis:

> Cast about rather for some good that will last.
> But there can be no such good except what the soul
> discovers for itself within itself. (EM I, 195)

No motivational techniques or trumpeted technologies of success will guarantee happiness, even if they do seem to work, when we are aiming at the wrong targets. And this is why it's important for the philosopher to advise us. Know thyself! Know thy good! And think through what you are tempted to chase before you pay the full price of pursuing and attaining it. This is great advice for us all.

INNER CONFIDENCE

As we develop the right sort of perspective on life, and proper goals for our energetic pursuit, we need an inner resilience to carry us through the hard times that life occasionally brings us all. In particular, Seneca believes that we need a resilient inner attitude of confidence in tackling the challenges and issues we'll inevitably face along the way. Only a state of inner resilience will put us into the best position to attain the outer results that we always hope to see from our efforts. The inner person is important to Seneca along these lines in two ways. It is the appropriate territory for our most essential focal goals, and it is the foundation for making our proper difference in the external world.

We get ourselves into trouble if we don't approach our daily challenges with the right inner attitudes. And at the core of the right attitudes is the positive state of confidence. Seneca remarks:

> Our lack of confidence doesn't come from difficulty;
> the difficulty comes from our lack of confidence.
> (EM III, 205)

Memorable. And quite often true. We frequently get ourselves into difficulties by moving forward without a stable confidence in our own trajectory. And those difficulties in turn further diminish our self-confidence, whose even lower level causes us to back off things we should be doing, and that then increases the overall trouble we face, which in turn is even more daunting, and so on, resulting in a downward spiral of unnecessary underachievement. Seneca believes that there is no good reason for this unfortunate process to get started. He expresses his own ideal by observing that:

CHAPTER 4

The wise man does not need to walk timidly and
with too much caution. His confidence in himself is
so great that he doesn't hesitate to stand up against
Fortune, and he will never retreat from her.
(ME II, 253)

Our guide insists that we are wisest not to be bullied by external happenstance, the ancient sense of the term translated here as
"Fortune." When we have our minds focused on a worthy goal, are
drawing on our real talents, and are building the inner conditions
of success within our own souls, we can block out the unnecessary
and debilitating worries that bind too many people. Properly charting our journeys to start with, adopting goals that are genuinely
right for us, can help tremendously with this. Seneca explains:

No change of fortune, and no external circumstance,
can shut off the wise man from action. The object
that engages his attention prevents his mind
from being captured by other things. He is ready
for either result: if goods, he controls them, and if
evils, he conquers them. (Ep. 307–09)

The thing that engages the wise man's attention is the goal he
is pursuing. That, our philosopher suggests, will minimize the intru-
sive impact of possible distractions and obstacles. The wise person
is ready for success or hardship at any turn in the road, and can
handle either as he moves farther in the direction of his ultimate
objectives.

Seneca concludes his description of the wise person's inner
response to external happenstance like this:

Nothing holds him back—not poverty, or pain, or
anything else that deflects the inexperienced and
pushes them around. Do you think he is weighed
down by evils? He makes use of them. (Ep. 307–09)

This is an exciting concept. The wise man builds on his successes, but he also makes use of his failures. The goods that come
and the setbacks are accepted and put to work, in one way or
another. The wise person does not worry about the exigencies of
fate, or run away from the prospect of trouble, but rather marches

ahead with the inner confidence that whatever happens can be handled and put to work for good.

The very difficulties that some people seek so assiduously to avoid end up being the testing ground for that vital state of mind known as self-knowledge. Seneca says:

> If a man is to know himself, he must be tested.
> No one finds out what he can do except by trying.
> (ME I, 25)

Too many people seem to view the toughness of the world, the difficulties of life, as undermining the possibility of any sort of strong confidence in our pursuits. Seneca looks at this in the opposite way, seeing the obstacles we face as a proving ground for that inner attitude of resilient self-confidence that we all need:

> The powers we have can never inspire in us a genuine inner self-confidence until we have confronted many difficulties along the way, and even now and then have had to struggle fiercely with them. This is the only way our true spirit ever can be really tested—the inner spirit we have that will never consent to be ruled by outer forces. The nature of such a spirit can be seen in the fact that no prizefighter can go into a contest with high spirits if he has never been beaten black and blue. The only man who can enter the ring with confidence is one who has seen his own blood, has felt his teeth rattled by an opponent's fist, has been tripped up and has experienced the full force of an adversary's charge, who has been knocked down in body but not in spirit —one who, as often as he falls, gets up again with greater determination than ever. (EM I, 75)

He even goes so far as to say in one place that:

> Disaster is virtue's opportunity. (ME I, 27)

In another passage, he explains that:

> While every sort of excess is harmful, the most dangerous of all is unlimited good fortune. (ME I, 31)

Modern medicine tells us that frequent colds can actually strengthen the immune system and bring us a physical hardiness we might not otherwise be able to attain. I've come across more than one instance where someone who seemed never to get sick suddenly developed a first illness and died. "He was never sick a day in his life," shocked friends and relatives say. But that was the problem. His body wasn't prepared to handle infection. Too much health can be bad for your health—as Yogi Berra might have said. Unlimited good fortune can make a person arrogant, and can make an organization complacent. People who haven't had to adjust and adapt to overcome failures and obstacles aren't as strong as those who have. Rather than deploring the negatives in life, Seneca sees them as conditions necessary for all the positives we need to bring into being. This world is a place of "soul making," as many great thinkers have commented, an arena for the building of character and the exercise of creative strength. Too much good fortune unfortunately encourages a lazy contentment more prone to comfort than courage. Unless the world kicks us in the pants now and then, we tend to be insufficiently motivated to become the best we are capable of being.

Speaking of the mind that can contemplate good and evil in these ways, Seneca admonishes:

> Let it have confidence in itself, rejoice in itself, admire its own resources, and withdraw as far as possible from the things of others. Let it devote itself to its own matters, not feel losses, and interpret in a positive way all adversities. (ME II, 267)

This is a philosopher well aware of the mind's crucial role in confidence building. The power of the mind is great. And, in particular, the power of our imaginations can hinder us, or help us along the way. Our imaginations are always moving beyond reality, either with fearful illusions or wonderful possibilities. We must take care to control this power. Seneca writes to a talented young friend:

> There are more things in this world, Lucilius, likely to frighten us than to crush us. We suffer more in imagination than in reality. (EM I, 75)

Plato had long before pointed out that things are not always what they seem. Seneca understands that if we don't control our imaginations and our emotional responses to events, they can come to control us, and lead us into false and unproductive conclusions. What we initially view as terrible can actually plant the seeds of good. Our philosopher picks up on this and pointedly asks:

> How often has what seemed to be terrible instead turned out to be the source and beginning of happiness? (EM III. 267)

The worst things I've ever been through have always somehow paved the way for the best things I've ever experienced. It's very strange. And yet it's true. So I try to keep this in mind whenever any situation coming my way looks bad. Things are not always what they seem. And even when they are, they may still lead to something very much better that we can't yet anticipate. We can use this insight to strengthen our emotions and support positive attitudes in apparently difficult circumstances.

It is up to us how we interpret the situations we face. Do we allow fear, insecurity, and other forms of negative thinking to hold us back, or do we choose instead to move boldly forward in the direction of our true potential? Do we portray our circumstances to ourselves as bleak and hopeless, or as an opportunity for creative invention, or extended persistence? Seneca goes so far as to say:

> There is no reason to believe that anything should be feared. (EM III. 267)

What an extraordinary claim this is. Our advisor is sure of this startling fact because of what he has learned from philosophy. He is utterly convinced that the biggest picture available from philosophy mitigates all our worries and puts everything into perspective. How then can we attain more confidence in our endeavors? Well, first we should allow philosophy to be our guide. The average person may be full of anxieties and uncertainties about any new challenge. So may the above average person. But it's precisely Seneca's claim that:

> Anyone who has practiced philosophy for
> inner health becomes as a result noble, confident,

unbeatable, and greater as you draw near him.
(EM III, 279)

Philosophy imparts an important form of understanding. If we
truly grasp the power of the mind and the soul over adversity, we
can free ourselves from unnecessary fear and enjoy the boldness
we need to move forward with judgment and power.

A second tactic for confidence building is suggested by philosophy to augment the impact of having a big picture within which
to handle both good and evil. Seneca believes that the best sort of
confidence is grounded in self-knowledge—a knowledge of our
strengths, certainly, but also a knowledge of our weaknesses. He
says:

> We are not all wounded at the same spot. You should
> know what your weak spot is so that you can be sure
> to protect it. (ME I, 281)

When you know your personal liabilities and weaknesses,
and can act so as to protect yourself from their vulnerability, you
have the basis for attaining a strength of reasonable confidence
suitable for the journey you face. And when you think through
the challenges you may have to face, anticipating them in
advance, and giving yourself a plan for handling them, you provide yourself with the strongest possible basis for confidence.
Seneca remarks:

> Everyone approaches a danger with more courage
> if he has prepared in advance how to confront it.
> Anyone can endure difficulties better if he has
> previously practiced how to deal with them. People
> who are unprepared can be unhinged by even the
> smallest of things. (EM III, 225)

Our philosopher recommends these strategies to us because of
the importance he attaches to confidence, or "faith," in all our
appropriate endeavors. Whether that faith will give us the real
progress we desire in attaining our goals in the outer world or not,
Seneca is sure that faith is important to have anyway. He even goes
so far as to say:

I don't know whether I'll make progress or not,
but I should prefer to lack success than to lack faith.
(EM I, 183)

Seneca seems to think that it is an intrinsic good to have faith
in yourself and your prospects in the world. It's just the right thing
to do. But of course, much more can be said as well. If we do have
that faith in ourselves and in the future of our projects, we render
it much more likely that we will make the progress we need and
have the success we hope for in all that we do.

5

PLANNING A LIFE

Proper goal setting is crucial for a successful life. So is an inner attitude of confidence. But Seneca, along with a chorus of other great thinkers, tells us that for success in difficult matters, where we have a challenging goal to attain, we all need to be planners as well as dreamers and believers.

Suppose you decide to grow a garden. You have from the start a clear idea in mind of what you want—a variety of vegetables clearly imagined. You generate within yourself an agricultural attitude of confident expectation—and then what? Well, you'd better get the equipment you need and buy some seeds. And then, put them in the ground. Obvious stuff if the topic is gardening, but these basic actions metaphorically represent the simple sequential steps that people often seem to omit in the more complex challenges of life and work.

The attainment of any complex or difficult goal requires strategy, initiative, adaptation, and learning along the way, with partners of many kinds. A focused concentration on what it will take to get the job done, a best assessment of all that might be needed from conception to achievement, is crucial. We need to plant our seeds and then get on with the rest of the plan. Seneca says:

> A farmer will lose everything he's planted if he
> stops working once the seed is in the ground.
> It takes a lot of care to bring crops to their yield.
> Nothing ever reaches the stage of fruit that's not
> nurtured by constant cultivation from the first day
> to the last. (ME III, 69)

Any exalted goal achievement is the culmination of a process of dynamic action, a process that requires planning, creativity, and continued hard work all along the way in support of a vision.

Seneca observes that many people fail to follow this simple wisdom for the art of life accomplishment. He writes:

> Some people follow no plan consistently but are pushed into one new scheme after another by a fickleness that's rambling, unstable, and never satisfied. Others have no goals at all but are just overtaken by fate as they stand and stare.
> (SPS 48)

Having a relatively stable set of objectives in life, or at any given stage of life, facilitates successful living. Planning consistently in support of those objectives is in turn a source of effective power.

There are no short cuts to the greatest forms of achievement. Worthy goals take very hard work. But this of course doesn't mean that our lives should be overflowing with non-stop exertion and frantic busyness every hour of every day. Seneca explains:

> A love of ceaseless activity is not diligence—it's just the restlessness of a driven mind. (EM I, 13)

Because of the fact that much is required of us by any challenging goal, we don't have time to waste on superfluous activities. The philosopher says:

> What do I encourage you to do? Nothing really novel —we're not trying to find cures for new evils—but this first of all: to see clearly for yourself what is necessary and what is superfluous. (EM III, 271)

How do we do that? How, in any situation, can we discern the difference between what is needed and what is not? Seneca has the simplest and most powerful possible answer:

> Look to your goal, in everything you do, and then you will get rid of superfluous things. (EM III, 373)

Seek first the kingdom—Eyes on the prize. From biblical pronouncements to the patter of the streets, we have this advice ensconced in our cultural wisdom. A clear conception of what is important, and of what we are seeking to make happen, will help us focus on what is necessary and what is not, at any stage of the process. And once we have determined a plan to get us from where we are to where we need to be, we must not hesitate to take action. Our man of thought and action urges us:

> Devote yourself to what should be done today, and you will not have to depend so much on tomorrow. (EM I, 3)

In any of life's challenges, the value of a plan can't be overstated. What is to be done today, and then what tomorrow? And yet our plans are not to be cast in stone. Even the best plans we develop are just intended to get us moving forward intelligently. They are not meant to straightjacket us and render us incapable of continued creative thinking. Seneca remarks, with the utmost of common sense:

> There is nothing wrong with changing a plan when the situation has changed. (ME III, 285)

Prepare for the challenge. Take action. And then adjust as you go forward. A plan is a rational tool for effective action, but it is only a tool. Seneca expands on his perspective, presenting adaptability as a sort of virtue midway between the opposite vices of stubbornness and fickleness. With any goal, we first need to chart out a plan of action, and then:

> We should work on being adaptable. Otherwise, we easily become too attached to plans we've already made. We need to be able to adjust to whatever conditions chance has given us, and not be afraid to change either our purpose or our position—as long as we don't let that flexibility become fickleness, a vice that won't give us any rest. (ME II, 267)

Life is balance, and that often requires holding ourselves poised between opposites. It is this sort of balance that is the key to our successful navigation of the shoals and sand bars of life.

Finally, we enhance our ability to plan and to adapt by consulting with the wisest advisors we can find. First, we need the wisdom of philosophers like Seneca, past and present, who can help us get our bearings. Those who understand the universality of the challenges we face in the deepest of senses can give us perspectives that will help us to maintain a wise course.

Then we should partner up with people whose particular skills and experience will aid us in our specific quest. We need to get to know people who can help us along in the process, who can assist in our planning and implementation. But as we interact with others, we must always be aware that their priorities are not often exactly the same as ours. If we do not keep this in mind, we easily fall victim to an erosion of our time and energy and find ourselves pressured to pursue activities that are off the course we've set ourselves and that are not at all in our own best interests.

Seneca is always harkening back to the issue of the precious nature of the time we have. In one passage that captures a wistful thought that is much like one many of us have at some point entertained, he writes:

> It was just a moment ago that I sat as a young man
> in the school of the philosopher Sotion, just a
> moment ago that I began to plead in the courts, just
> a moment ago that I lost the desire to plead, and just
> a moment ago that I lost the ability. The flight of
> time is infinitely swift, as those see more clearly
> who are looking back. (EM I, 323)

He then says:

> This is the reason I'm all the more angry that
> some men claim most of this time for superfluous
> things—time that, no matter how carefully we guard
> it, is never quite enough even for necessary things.
> (EM I, 325)

We must learn to plan, and then to implement those plans day to day, not allowing the temptations of diversion and distraction to derail us from the best use of one of the most valuable of our resources, time. We should always seek to collaborate with and learn from people who can help us in the journey, but finally, we must stay in charge of our own journey of life success to the extent that we can, guarding the time that we have, and using it well.

CONSISTENT LIVING

In line with other great Stoic thinkers, Seneca views the quality of consistency as crucial for any life, and for any quest within life's journey. In the course of giving a list of the most important virtues for human life, he remarks:

> There is also steadfastness, that cannot be dislodged from its position, and cannot be made to abandon its purpose by any exertion of force. (Ep, 41)

Steadfastness is a form of consistency in pursuing a goal or in living out a vision. It is one of the most universal conditions for satisfying achievement in any endeavor.

Seneca realizes how difficult consistency often seems to be, but he insists on its importance. He writes these harsh words of admonition to a friend, words many of us need to hear:

> Your greatest difficulty is in yourself. You are your own biggest obstacle. You don't know what you want. You're better at approving the right course than at following it. You see where the true happiness lies, but you don't have the courage to attain it. (EM I, 141)

This is well said. Inconsistency often shows that at some level we really don't know what we want. At other times, it show that we don't have the courage of our convictions. Our avowed goals point in one direction. Our behavior points in another. And yet we often fool ourselves into thinking that our troubles are caused wholly by external circumstances. Seneca says:

Why do we fool ourselves? The evil that harms us
most is not external, but internal, lodged deep inside
us. As long as we don't realize we're sick, it's just
that much harder for us to attain proper health.
(EM I, 333)

Inconsistency of thought and behavior is one of the most common
causes of failure in our world. It is also one of the most unac-
knowledged. But the force of inconsistency is directly self-defeating, and often self-destructive. The inconsistent person is his own
worse enemy. Our Stoic sage tells us that:

You can curse a man with no heavier curse than
to pray that he will be at odds with himself.
(EM III, 267)

Inconsistent behavior is a curse, but it isn't just that—it's also
something of an enigma. Seneca puzzles over it like many of us do,
and writes to his friend:

What is this force, Lucilius, that drags us in one
direction when we really want to go in another,
urging us on to the very same place we want to
leave? What is it that wrestles with our spirit and
won't let us desire anything consistently? We jump
from one plan to another. None of our wishes is
free, none is unqualified, and none of them is
lasting. (EM I, 345)

Whatever the ultimate explanation might be for the power and
pervasiveness of inconsistency in human life, Seneca stands firm on
his recommendation. Consistency is crucial. He urges:

Make progress, and, before all else, try hard to be
consistent with yourself. (EM I, 245)

"Before all else"—That is a very strong phrase. Elsewhere, he adds:

It is indeed consistency that will last—false things do
not. (EM III, 393)

Consistency is truth. Inconsistency is falsehood. This is an interesting and powerful concept. When you act consistently, you are true to yourself. An inconsistent act is falsely related to your deepest goals and values, and, as such, will not have any positive lasting value. Seneca sees consistency as central to making each of us singular, whole, integrated people. He says:

> Believe me, it is a great role—to play the part of one man. But nobody can be one person except the wise man. The rest of us shift our masks. (EM III, 395)

Inconsistency is a shift of mask. You present yourself to the world as being other than who you are. Seneca thinks of it as very important that we appear to be exactly who we are, and that we live who we are steadfastly. He cleverly advises:

> See to it that men are able to praise you—and if they won't do that, make sure they can at least identify you. (EM III, 395)

No one really knows who the inconsistent man or woman really is. Consistency, persistence, and steadfastness are determinative virtues of character, and, when joined to the right goals and values, are conditions for lasting success in the world.

Our philosopher sometimes positions consistency in terms of one of the deepest concepts in either Eastern or Western thought, the idea of harmony. He recommends:

> Make sure that all your actions and words harmonize and fit with each other, and are stamped in the same mold. If a man's actions are out of harmony, his soul is crooked. (EM I, 243)

With an anecdote alluding to an individual well known and admired in his time, he emphasizes the ultimate importance of consistent or harmonious behavior in little things as well as in big ones:

> Marcus Agrippa, a man of great soul and the only person raised to fame and power by the civil wars whose prosperity helped the state, used to say that

he owed a lot to the proverb "Harmony makes small
things grow, and a lack of harmony makes great
things decay." (EM III, 41)

Generalizing, Seneca further maintains that

Philosophy teaches us to act, and not just to speak.
It demands of everyone that he should actually
live by his own standards, that his life should not
be out of harmony with his words, and that his
inner existence should be of one hue, and fully
harmonious with all his outer activities. This, I say,
is the highest duty and the highest proof there is
of real wisdom—that deed and word should be in
accord, that a man should be equal to himself under
all conditions, and that he always should be the
same. (EM I, 135)

The most common causes of inconsistency or discord among
our actions are transitory and often irrational emotional and mental states like fear, temptation, anger, laziness, or distraction.
Seneca believes that the best preventive medicine is rightly
applied reason:

Reason should be our guide. All our actions, from
the smallest to the greatest, must follow her lead.
As she directs, we should do. (ME III, 87)

Reason is not for Seneca any thin intellectual matter. It is the
whole ability we have to grasp, through intuition, interpretation,
and inference, what the truth is about anything Reason will show
us where inconsistency lies and how we can avoid it. It may take
a lot more than reason to help us break bad habits of inconsistent
action; we may have to use our imaginations and cultivate the right
emotions to dislodge the power of our irrational impulses, but our
efforts should always be guided and instigated by the dictates of
reason, which alone can inform us what is and is not in our own
best interests.

Consider, for instance, what our philosopher says about anger,
which he calls "the most hideous and frenzied of the emotions",
and further characterizes as a "temporary madness" (ME I, 107). He
gives advice like this:

> The best course is to reject at once the first
> incitement to anger, to resist even its small
> beginnings, and work hard not to fall into it. If
> it even begins to lead us astray, a return to the safe
> path is difficult. Whenever we allow this emotion
> in, and by our own free choice let it rule, reason
> becomes powerless. After that, the anger will do,
> not just what you allow it, but whatever it chooses.
> (ME I, 125)

The irritants in life are all around us. Frustrations can ambush us at any turn. Perceived slights, blatant insults, deceptions, betrayals, rude behavior and other injustices can take us by surprise at any time. But we shouldn't let them get to us. In another place, Seneca asserts quite vividly:

> He is a great and noble man who acts like the lordly
> wild beast and listens with no real concern to the
> baying of tiny dogs. (ME I, 239)

Our advisor makes the point often made by Socrates and others that negative emotions like anger recoil upon their host, and that this alone should give us sufficient motivation to block their onslaught:

> Won't everyone be glad to block any impulse to
> anger when he realizes that it begins by working
> harm, first of all, to him? (ME I, 263)

But realizing that we may need some backup advice when it comes to anything as powerful as anger, Seneca says:

> In my opinion, however, there are only two rules—
> not to fall into anger, and in anger to do no wrong.
> (ME I, 203)

Our Stoic sage urges again and again that we should have a touchstone of truth in our lives to help us control those forces that otherwise can lead us astray and defeat us. He counsels:

> You should embrace firmly—once and for all—a sin-
> gle ethical standard to live by, and then you should
> regulate your whole life by it. (EM I, 135)

With a governing principle, a clear conception of what we want, of what we value, and of how we mean to go about it all, we have in our possession what it takes to identify and resist any impulse that would derail our progress through life.

Seneca basically believes that we have no time for inconsistent behavior. And he thinks too few of us understand this. He says:

> Can you show me anyone who places any value on his time, realizes the worth of each day, and understands that he is dying daily? (EM I, 3)

The time we have is not to be wasted or squandered in self-defeating activities. But distractions are all around us. He writes to his young friend:

> Nothing, Lucilius, really belongs to us but time. Nature gave us ownership of this one thing, so fleeting and hard to hold on to that anyone who tries can take it away from us. (EM I, 5)

Because of this, he implores us to use all our available energy:

> We should work hard with all the courage we can muster, ignoring any distractions, and struggle with a single purpose. Otherwise, when we're left behind, we'll realize too late the speed of quick-flying time, whose passing we cannot slow. We should greet each day when it comes, as being the best, and make it our own possession. (EM III, 247)

And again he says:

> Let us take possession of all the time available to us. This, however, cannot happen unless we first take possession of our own selves. (Ep. 95)

We can make the time of each day our possession, we can take ownership of it, by charting out our actions consistently with our goals and values, by resisting attractive but distracting and destructive alternative options, and by allowing our inner person to flow harmoniously into the world. But this takes work and daily assessment. In that regard, Seneca remarks:

> Sextius had this habit, at the end of the day when he had retired to his nightly rest, to ask his soul these questions: "What bad habit have you cured today? What fault have you resisted? In what way are you better?" (ME I, 341)

If we work hard to attain consistency with our deepest goals and values, to make the most of the time we have on this earth each day, we will move ourselves farther in the direction of our proper life achievement. It's up to us how we use each hour. Are we consistent or scattered? Are we disrupted or in harmony? It's all ultimately up to us. As long as we blame circumstances for our problems, we continue to create the greatest of those problems. When we take responsibility and take action consistently with our sense of purpose, we reclaim what is rightfully ours, and position ourselves for doing the good we are here in this world to do. This is a vitally important aspect of the Stoic art of living.

THE HEART

The Stoic philosophers were extremely concerned about how we tend to react to difficulties and obstacles along our path. When things don't go as we would like, when life seems to deal us a blow, we too often feel such emotions as irritation, frustration, anger, despondency, despair, depression, and gloom. We are shaken, anxious, fearful, and jealous of others who seem to be better treated by the world. And that, the Stoics say, shows that we are far too dependent on externals for our equilibrium and happiness. Our thoughts, emotions, attitudes, and actions should be under the governance of reason, should be rooted in our own inner nobility of character, and therefore should not be subject to the vicissitudes of Fortune. Seneca explains that:

> The happy man is not that person the crowd considers happy, namely, the one who has huge amounts of money flowing his way, but rather is a man whose true possessions are all in his soul. He is upright and noble, spurns inconstancy, would trade places with no one, and esteems men only at their value as men. He takes nature as his teacher, conforms to her laws, and lives as she commands. No violence can steal what he has—he turns evil into good, is unerring in his judgment, is unshaken by events, and lives without fear. He may be moved by force but is never moved to distraction. When Fortune with all her might throws at him her deadliest missile, he may be grazed, though rarely, but is never wounded. (EM 295–97)

The Stoics all counseled us to steel ourselves against the onslaughts of disturbing emotions. And, from their distinctive point of view, elation can be as bad as depression, equally unhinging our reason and deflecting our conduct from the proper paths we ought to take. Surely, in this they were right, however surprising the thought initially might seem. Any extreme of emotion can distort our perspective if it gets out of control. Most of us have had the experience of doing things we later have difficulty owning up to because of such extreme emotions as excitement out of control, or runaway fear. Expressing the wise man's point of view, Seneca writes:

> Nature intended that no great equipment should be necessary for happiness. Each one of us is able to make himself happy. External things are of very little importance and actually have no great influence either way. The wise man is not elated by external prosperity or depressed by outer adversity, and this is because he tries always to rely mainly on himself and to find all his joy within himself. (ME II, 425)

The impact of negative emotion is undeniable. That's why the Stoics had a great deal to say about how to deal with it. But they also warned us about any experience of an emotion, in itself negative or positive in feel, that might get out of control and take us in a direction at cross purposes with our true good. And these warnings are important. Irrational exuberance can derail us from a proper course just as powerfully as unreasonable despair. Any emotion that runs out of control can unhinge us and thwart our progress in life. That is a realization for which the Stoic philosophers are particularly well known. But we also need to attend to any insight they might have about any possible healthy role that positive emotion might play in our lives.

The most insightful thinking about life success in recent years has pointed to the important role of passion, or robust emotional commitment, in all long-term success. In the seventeenth century, Blaise Pascal, the French scientist and mathematician who was greatly influenced in many ways by earlier Stoic thought, penned the memorable claim that: "The heart has its reasons of which reason knows nothing." Yet the view that these reasons of the heart can play a positive role in life is not a sentiment normally associated with the Stoic point of view.

Stoic philosophers are notorious for attempting to minimize the importance of emotion in our lives. It's almost as if they are so intent on freeing us from enslavement to negative emotions that they are far too leery of positive ones as well. They stress repeatedly and emphatically the proper role of reason in life, but they by contrast say very little about the potentially good effects of any proper and well-directed passion.

We have to look carefully throughout the body of Seneca's work to discern his true realization of the role that emotional commitment should play in any quest for success in life. Consider, for example, the following rare passage:

> Anything that isn't perfect is unsteady, sometimes getting better, and sometimes worse. Such a thing will certainly slide backward unless it keeps pushing ahead. If a man eases up in zeal and faithful application, he inevitably falls back. And no one can resume his progress exactly where he left off. Therefore, we should press on and persevere. There is much more of the road ahead of us than there is behind us, but the greater part of progress is the desire to progress. (Ep. 95)

Here Seneca affirms the importance of zeal, or passionate commitment, to making ongoing progress in meeting our challenges and in living our lives. He even goes so far as to say that, "the greater part of progress is the desire to progress." Without a positive desire to animate us, goal setting, confidence building, and any efforts of planning can end up being no more than empty, futile exercises. Passion is the fuel of the soul.

Ideally, a Stoic affirmation of passion might go something like this. With a proper exercise of human reason, in its deeply intuitive function, we can recognize great goods that we can and should pursue. And when we set ourselves a goal that captures the realization of any such good, we give ourselves a positive ground of emotional motivation throughout our whole being. Seneca insists that:

> The good stimulates the mind, and in a way, molds and embraces what is essential to the body. (EM III, 219)

The good we pursue acts as a mental and physical stimulus. Think about it for a minute. When you are excited about your pursuit of some great good, you're more eager to get up in the morning, you have a spring in your step, your mind is more alert, and your whole body seems energized. When you're not on the trail of such a good, you often languish, physically and mentally. That's why, in any endeavor of goal setting and planning, whether professional or personal, it's so important to point out, to ourselves and to others, the connections that exist between our targets and those goods we so deeply embrace. The good, as Plato might say, is the true, and it is the beautiful. And it excites our passion in its pursuit.

Seneca observes:

> This is the most excellent attribute the noble soul
> has within itself, that it can be roused to honorable
> things. (EMI, 261)

Consider this striking claim carefully. The single most excellent quality the noble soul has within itself is, surprisingly for this Stoic thinker, not reason but the capacity for being "roused to honorable things." And what is the state of arousal to honorable things but an emotional commitment to the importance of we are doing in working toward the attainment of those things?

A sense of nobility in what we are doing is the only lasting source of motivation in work or in life. A loftiness in our own conception of our journey is crucial to its success and to its ongoing excellence. But Seneca is quick to point out that the noble and emotionally committed individual is not arrogant or presumptuous about what he or she is doing. Personal humility is perfectly compatible with the sort of nobility of attitude we are talking about in this connection. In fact, Seneca remarks:

> The difference between a lofty and a haughty soul,
> I say, is great. (ME I, 161)

This philosopher sees all proper journeys of life success as quests for wisdom and virtue, as well as for the good that these states of being can accomplish. And when he contemplates the essence of the adventure that we are here on this earth to undertake, he is moved in his innermost passions. He remarks to a close friend:

> I fully understand what this task is. It's something
> that I desire, and I want it with all my heart. I see
> that you also have been aroused and are hastening
> with great zeal towards infinite beauty. (Ep. 95)

In the end, Seneca does recognize with Pascal something of the importance of the heart. We are to respond to life with reason and zeal. The heart and the mind must work together.

This is our calling, and nothing less. Everything we do should serve infinite goodness and infinite truth, which together amount to infinity beauty. That nobility of task is alone able to spur us on to the highest and deepest emotional commitment to the importance of any job we find at hand. Ultimately, the inner foundations for happiness and the good life are not just intellectual, but involve properly directed passion as well.

THE ETHICS OF
CHARACTER

All the Stoic philosophers emphasized the importance of character and virtue to a good and happy life. Seneca joins a crowd of like-minded philosophers when he asserts that success in life should be thought of and sought after only as an outcome of personal goodness and ethical strength, and should never be pursued in its absence. He advises:

> It's a good thing to have this as your goal, or your ideal: to be considered the greatest man only if at the same time you are considered the best. (ME I, 415)

For Seneca, issues of moral character are central to the living of a good life. In speaking of servants, he says in one passage:

> I intend to value them in reference to their character, and not according to their duties. (EM I, 309)

But this is an altogether general perspective. According to the Stoic point of view, all people should be viewed and valued in accordance with their inner character rather than in response to any of their external circumstances.

In addition to those passages in Seneca's writings where goodness and character are praised, there are just as many where wrongdoing is condemned. Echoing the views of his greatest predecessors, Seneca characterizes unethical conduct not only as evil, but, in addition, as self-destructive. He says:

> When we do wrong, only the least and slightest bit of it flows over to our neighbor. The worst and, if I

> may use the term, the densest portion of it stays at
> home and troubles its owner. (Ep, 233–35)

The unethical individual makes himself a bad person. And he creates for himself bad circumstances. For, as Aristotle had warned us, when we treat others badly we must always be concerned that they are out there in the world preparing to do harm to us in return. Seneca writes:

> The most important contribution to peace of mind
> is never to do wrong. Those who lack self-control
> lead disturbed and tumultuous lives. Their crimes are
> matched by their fears, and they are never at peace.
> (EM III, 216–17)

In our concern to take the high road in life, we must be continually aware that everything counts. No action or decision is too small to be exempt from the moral perspective. Nothing is insignificant. Seneca says:

> If you pay close attention, all actions are significant.
> You can judge character by even the very smallest
> signs. (EM I, 351)

The ubiquity of the ethical is mirrored by its accessibility. Seneca writes that:

> Although in other things there are great distinctions
> of rank and birth, virtue is available to everyone.
> She thinks no man unworthy if only he thinks
> himself worthy of her. (ME II, 407)

If then character is so important, if virtue is in principle available to us all, and if ethical action is the only foundation for secure and lasting success, we are naturally led to ask how we can move toward greater ethical sensitivity in our own lives, and farther into deeper levels of character development. Our philosopher of the inner life has an answer. He tells us first of all that:

> Nothing is more successful in having a positive
> influence on the mind, or in straightening out a

> wavering spirit prone to evil, than association
> with good men. Seeing often what they do and
> hearing frequently what they say makes an
> impression on the heart and creates a powerful
> influence. (EM III, 37)

We become like the people we are around. This seems to be a universal truth recognized by the wisest people in every culture. Therefore, Seneca concludes, we should seek the companionship of good people.

And, of course, we can benefit from finding ourselves on either side of that process. Seneca advises us in a two-fold way:

> Associate with people who will make you a better
> human being. And welcome those you can improve.
> The process is mutual, for men learn while they
> teach. (EM I, 35)

It's not just that we should seek out saints and sages to emulate. We ourselves should be prepared to teach others the high road of virtuous character.

This can strike a chord of novelty in many business contexts today, where everything but ethics is a normal part of daily conversation. We talk numbers and teach both tactics and techniques, but we feel awkward about trying to teach or learn more concerning the most important issues of life. We rob ourselves as well as others of the good that could be ours if we would just allow ethical issues and matters of character onto the radar screen of our consciousness and into the rhythms of our conversation.

Seneca believes that we should have moral heroes in our lives, whether people near to us, or remote in space or time. We should watch and emulate those whose goodness we find most impressive. We learn to be what we fix our attention upon. In one passage he says:

> Choose for yourself a moral hero whose life,
> conversation, and expressive face all please you,
> then picture him to yourself at all times as your
> protector, and as your ethical pattern. We all need
> someone whose example can help us regulate our
> characters. You can never correct something
> crooked without a ruler. (EM I, 65)

He also approvingly quotes the philosopher Epicurus as having said:

> Cherish some man of great character, and keep him always in mind. Then live as if he were watching you, and order all your actions as if he saw them. (EM I, 65)

Both passages together give us a double dose of advice about putting to use an inner mental picture of an admirable moral character. With the use of this moral image, we are to:

Emulate

and

Regulate

We are to emulate the moral strength of character that our image of a revered mentor provides and regulate our own choices by means of that inner vision of a good man or woman. Seneca is recognizing here the extraordinary power of imprinting, or imitation in human life. As a part of our own moral growth, he advises us to imitate the actions and reactions of that particular person we deeply admire, and pattern ourselves on what we imagine this individual would do in the same situation we now face. Likewise, he uses the words of Epicurus to suggest, we should regulate our decisions at another level by asking what our moral hero or exemplar would say if he or she were to see us acting in the way we contemplate.

This latter advice is a version of what has sometimes been called "The Publicity Test" for ethical decision making: What would I do if I knew my actions and intentions would become front page news, or would be completely revealed to my spouse, or children, or my most admired teacher? In another place Seneca urges:

> Live among men as if God saw you, and speak with God as if men were listening. (EM I, 59)

In all our morally relevant decision-making, we should imagine ourselves observed and judged by the most perfect moral being of all. And when we address this being, we should imagine our prayers broadcast for all to hear. This is an especially interesting double test, meant to encourage propriety in secret as well as in public.

We often think of ethics as if it's a matter of numerous and complex rules for what and to do and what not to do in every conceivable situation. In modern times we are encouraged to suspect that ethical dilemmas will stalk us at every turn, making it nearly impossible to have agreed upon, universally applicable standards for our professional and personal behavior. Seneca, however, thinks ethical living is basically quite simple. He concludes:

> This is the core of my advice: Treat those below you as you would want to be treated by those above you. (EM I, 307)

This is, of course, an interesting version of the famous Golden Rule. Seneca, as a man accustomed to political hierarchy, is not too worried about advising anyone on how to relate to superiors. We are, for the most part, naturally deferential and solicitous toward those on whose good will our careers and even lives depend. Our astute ethical advisor would instead turn our attention to the reverse relation and focus us on how we treat those who depend on us, who work for us, and who report to us. How do we treat the people around us who are not in a position of power over us? How do we act toward those who are not, in some sense, our peers or social equals? Seneca believes that we should imagine ourselves in their place and act toward them as we would have people correspondingly positioned over us to act toward us.

This is an unusual employment of Golden Rule thinking that encourages us always to imagine ourselves in a subordinate position. And this maneuver is connected in a powerfully deep way with Seneca's Big Picture for all of human life. He sees us as ultimately standing in reciprocally dependent relations with each other, across all hierarchical status and power barriers. He thinks of us all as mutually dependent in a deep cosmic sense. In opposition to the self-absorbed individualism that dominates our age and makes ethics so challenging in the modern world, Seneca writes:

> There is no such thing as good fortune or bad fortune for the individual alone. We all live in common. No one can live happily who thinks only of himself and transforms everything into

a question of his own good. You must live for
your neighbor, if you want to live for yourself.
(EM I, 315)

Using a vivid image, he writes further that:

Our relations with one another are like a stone
arch, which would collapse if the stones did not
mutually support each other, and which is held
up in this very way. (EM III, 91)

This is the moral and metaphysical vision needed for the greatest form of partnership and collaboration in human life. Human
interdependency is a fundamental fact of life and should govern
how we think of morality and ethics in our attitudes and actions
toward each other. Seneca concludes:

I can lay down a rule for mankind, in short
compass, for our duties in human relationships:
All that you see, all that encompasses both God
and man, is one—we are all parts of one great
body. (EM III, 91)

Our success in life should always be conceived, and evaluated,
while keeping this firmly in mind.

9

SEIZING THE DAY

Joining a chorus of philosophical voices through the centuries, Seneca believes that for sustainable success in life, we need to cultivate a capacity to enjoy the process or journey along the way to the realization of our goals.

Too many people, in their fixation on success, paradoxically undermine their own ability to experience it wholly. They sacrifice the quality of today for the uncertain rewards of tomorrow and become mired in habits of thought and feeling that make it difficult to enjoy any aspect of the process. Now, of course, we often need to be able to engage in some form of self-sacrifice or self-discipline for long-term benefits, but this is compatible with a general policy of enjoying each day as much as possible while it's here, compatible with our other commitments and the necessities of providing for a good tomorrow. Here is the danger, Seneca says:

> Consider individuals, survey human beings in general—there is no one whose life does not look forward to tomorrow. "What harm is there in this?" you ask. Infinite harm, for such people never live, but are always just preparing to live. (EM I, 299)

Proper human achievement, or success in life, is a process to be lived and enjoyed at as many stages in the journey as possible. We should never allow planning to displace living. Hope should never totally defer enjoyment.

There is another problem. Too many people seem to find it impossible to enjoy the present just because of some possible difficulties they anticipate in the future. Seneca points to the lack of wisdom in this approach to life by saying:

> It's really foolish to be unhappy now because you
> may be unhappy at some future time. (EM I, 167)

Carpe Diem! Seize the day! An enjoyment of the present should be
a proper part of our foundation for success in the future. "But what
if the day is full of troubles?" we easily ask. It is never so full of
troubles as to be bereft of good. That is the Stoic view. We strength-
en ourselves to overcome the troubles we face when we refresh
ourselves with a reminder of, and an ability to relish, whatever
goods we do have in our lives at any tough time. Even during the
most difficult of challenges, and the hardest of work, there is something that can be enjoyed. The Stoics believe it is up to us whether
we see it, and allow ourselves to experience that measure of enjoyment available to us, however great or small.

As the wisest people have always known, work and play are
not diametrically opposed. A serious person need not be somber.
Seneca illustrates by telling us:

> Socrates did not blush to play with little children.
> (ME II, 279)

We are too burdened by our ambitions, too worried by irritations,
fears, and disappointments. We need to take charge of our inner
attitudes and innermost experience, freeing ourselves of the negatives that hold us back, and embracing the moment we have on
earth. Seneca says:

> In any kind of life you will find that there are
> amusements and relaxations and pleasures if you
> are willing to consider your evils lightly rather
> than to make them terrible. (ME II, 249)

It is ultimately we ourselves who determine whether our evils, the
bad things that we cannot avoid, are sources of great suffering, or
merely potholes on the road of life. How do we react day to day?
What do we focus on? Amusements, relaxations and small pleas-
ures are out there awaiting our openness. So are exquisite joys.
And they can help us to achieve our deepest dreams.

The great irony is that pushing too much for success makes our
greatest success less likely. It is only the relaxed and rested mind

that can be intuitive and creative to its highest potential. Our doctor of the soul tells us:

> The mind should be given a rest. It will arise
> better and sharper after relaxing. As fertile fields
> should not be forced—since without rest, their
> productiveness will soon exhaust them—so
> constant work will break the strength of the mind.
> But if it's relaxed and rested a little while, it will
> recover its powers. Constant mental toil creates
> in the mind a kind of sluggishness and fatigue.
> (ME II, 281)

A sixteen or eighteen hour workday is not necessarily the key to success.

Again, Seneca continues:

> We should take care of the mind, and occasionally
> give it the leisure that serves as its food and
> strength. In addition, we should take walks outside
> so that that the mind can be strengthened and
> refreshed by being outdoors as we breathe the fresh
> air. Sometimes it will get new vigor from a trip by
> carriage and a change of place, along with festive
> company and generous drinking. (ME II, 283)

Take a walk, have a cool drink, slow down at your next meal and savor each bite, go see a movie with friends, visit a club, get on a bike and take a ride. Enjoy yourself! Refresh yourself! This is not just a matter of taking a break from your proper business in life; it's meant to be an important part of the process itself.

Advising his young friend who is quickly merging onto the fast lane and is thus in danger of becoming a driven, workaholic personality fixated on future achievement, Seneca writes in a letter:

> Above all, my dear Lucilius, make this your
> business: learn how to feel joy. (EM I, 161)

He adds in another place:

> Joy is an elation of spirit—of a spirit that trusts
> in the goodness and truth of its own possessions.
> (EMI, 411)

Joy comes from within. It is a response of the spirit that relies on the intrinsic value of its own inner resources—its wisdom and virtue, its talents and potential. Those are its only genuine possessions. Real joy does not depend on the external world, but reflects the richness of the spirit into that world. The deeply joyous person is a person of great inner strength. And the joyous person is more likely to see great results in the outer world as well.

Joy is an important part of the happy life. And it is an important part of the life of true achievement. Seneca is absolutely convinced that, ultimately, it is up to each of us what quality of life we live, and what we experience as a result of it. Whatever happens around us and to us in this world, we have within ourselves all the resources that we need. He remarks:

> The soul is more powerful than any sort of fortune.
> By its own agency, it guides its affairs in either
> direction, and out of its own power can produce a
> happy life, or a wretched one. (EM III, 119)

And, so, this doctor of the soul prescribes for all of us that inner work on wisdom and virtue that will take us to the quality of life we need and are here to experience in this magnificent world.

INNER ACHIEVEMENT AND PERSONAL FREEDOM

Epictetus on the Life Worth Living

10

THE LIBERATOR OF
THE SOUL

Epictetus was a slave. But, then, he thought that most of us are too. We are slaves to fashion, as well as to the opinions of neighbors, friends, relatives, our employers, the stock market, and our business associates. We are enslaved by a lifestyle, dependent on money, and even on increasing amounts of it, hassled through the day by the demands of a career, or driven to distraction by just sheer busyness. Our time is not our own. Some of our values can even seem imposed on us. We have hopes for our children, plans for ourselves, and worries about tomorrow. In a thousand ways, our sense of wellbeing, and our personal experience of happiness, depend on things outside our control. We pray for luck and health and peace, and dread the exigencies of disease, calamity, and death.

Epictetus believed we need liberation from all the forces that enslave us. And he was convinced that the freedom we need is to be found by following the guidance of Stoic philosophy.

For Epictetus, the Stoic art of living, the art of inner resilience, was no mere intellectual curiosity. It was his life-jacket in a sea of trouble. It kept him afloat and carried him from the crashing waves of his own problems to the distant shores of personal freedom, inner peace, and philosophical greatness. This, he believed, was genuine achievement.

We don't know too many details of his life, but we do have enough information to see that it was indeed remarkable. Epictetus came into this world in about the year A.D. 55 and died around A.D. 135. He was born in what is now Turkey, grew up as a slave, and was brought to Rome in the service of Epaphroditus, who was one of the Emperor Nero's personal bodyguards.

At the time, it was fashionable for wealthy or highly positioned slave owners to send their servants to school to become experts in various arts and sciences. Epaphroditus accordingly sent Epictetus to study philosophy with Musonius Rufus, a famous Stoic teacher at the time. The perspective of Stoicism was perfect for Epictetus. It caused him to look within and discover all his real personal power. It offered him a view of true human greatness, and liberated his thinking. It proved to him that no one can subjugate and enslave what is most vital about our lives. And it gave him a vision for what constitutes the greatest human good: the inner character that we cultivate, the full mental perspective that we bring to any external situation, and a virtue of the soul that can withstand any difficulty or suffering with true nobility.

What else we know about this philosopher can be enumerated quite simply. We are told that he was in some way crippled from an early age. He was eventually released from slavery and became an independent teacher of philosophy. He lived most of his life alone, and had few possessions. When the Emperor Domition expelled all philosophers from Rome in A.D. 89, Epictetus went to Nicopolis, near the shore, and opened an informal school for philosophy that was visited over a period of years by a great many people, including a number of politically important individuals, and even a subsequent Emperor.

Late in life, this independent Stoic thinker took it upon himself to adopt an infant boy who had been left to die by a poor family. He then also invited a woman he knew into his home to help care for the child, either as a nurse or as a surrogate mother.

Our philosophical guide never wrote down his own thoughts for posterity. He spent his time engaged in lively conversations with students and visitors each day. Fortunately for us, a perceptive and talented young man named Arrian took copious notes on many of these talks. He was later to be known by scholars for his historical writings on Alexander the Great. Arrian arranged his notes on the thoughts of Epictetus into eight books of "Discourses," many involving lively exchanges between the philosopher and a conversation partner. Four of these books survived and have been handed down to us. Arrian also compiled short nuggets of his teacher's wisdom into a Manual for Living, *The Encheiridion*, which we also possess.

Throughout these reported conversations and wisdom sayings, Epictetus comes across as a single-minded liberator of the human spirit. He talks straight, takes on the toughest topics, and surprises us now and then by cracking a joke right in the middle of a serious argument. Epictetus was a true evangelist for the Stoic philosophy of life. He uplifts us, cajoles us, rebukes us, and makes us think. But most of all, he wants to change the way we live.

As we begin to read what he has to say, we need to be confronted first with these challenging words:

> Why do you ever choose to read? Tell me. If it's only for entertainment, or just to learn something, you're a silly and lazy individual. But if you read for the right purpose, what else is this than to attain a peaceful and happy life? If reading does not gain you a peaceful and happy life, then what is the point of it? (IV.4.4)

Epictetus wanted to help us attain happiness in our lives. He believed this is the personal achievement that matters most. He couldn't give it to us as a gift, but he could assist us in seeing what changes we might need to make in order to bring it into our lives. He presents his mission, and our job, like this:

> Now I am your teacher and you are learning in my school. I have this purpose: to complete you, to free you from restraint, compulsion, hindrance, to make you free, prosperous, and happy, looking to God in everything, small and great. And you are here to learn and practice these things. (II.19.29)

Epictetus had learned the art of life achievement from acknowledged masters. And he encourages us to do so as well. We live in a world of talkers. But we all need to become productive listeners, directing our attention to the wisdom of those perceptive thinkers around us who might be a little farther down life's road than we are, and to those who, like Epictetus, carry the reports of other such sages to us. He declares:

> Nature has given to each of us one tongue, but two ears, so that we may hear from others twice as much as we speak. (F.CXLII)

When we hear the voice of Epictetus, as it echoes in his words, we always learn. This practical thinker was eager to pass along his insights to anyone who would be willing to listen and change.

Arrian himself testifies to the power that Epictetus had in person. The awed student wrote of this great teacher in his introduction to the Discourses that

> He had no other purpose than to move the minds
> of his listeners to the best things. If, indeed,
> these Discourses should produce that effect, they
> will have, I think, the result that the words of
> philosophers should have. But if they do not, let
> those who read them know that, when Epictetus
> spoke them, the listener could not escape being
> moved in the way that Epictetus wanted him to be.
> But if the Discourses as written here do not have this
> result, it could be that it's completely my fault, or it
> might be that this is just unavoidable. (Lines 5–8)

Arrian should not have worried. Across all the centuries, the words he recorded still have the power to change lives. They will, of necessity, affect anyone who comes to them with a desire for happiness, anyone who aspires to liberation from those forces that bind us and hold us back. Whether in person or on the page, the Stoic philosophy of Epictetus, with its distinctive art of living, has the capacity to redirect our thinking to great things in new and fulfilling ways.

11

PHILOSOPHY AND HAPPINESS

It's the first day of class, in a randomly selected college or university in America. You settle into your seat and await the arrival of the professor. You've heard that philosophy would be a good course to take, and that it might enhance your understanding of life. So your anticipation is keen.

The philosopher appears. You can tell because he is the only one in the room with a ratty old briefcase, a tangled beard, and a facial expression somehow caught between purposeful and lost. He's wearing a rumpled jacket, wrinkled khaki pants, a shirt buttoned wrong, and scuffed-up, old shoes. He puts his briefcase on the desk up front, emits a world weary sigh, and says, to no one in particular: "Good morning class. I am your professor for the semester." And, turning as if to go write on the board, he stops, twists back to face the room, and rhetorically, almost wistfully, asks: "But who am I, really? The "I" that is your professor, the "I" who speaks to you now—Who or what is this "I"? What is the meaning of the word 'I'?" He strokes his beard and looks perplexed.

Forty eight minutes later, hammered into near insensibility with seemingly endless questions about the meanings of the word "I" and "we," and language about "the soul," along with some rambling tangential asides about the moronic administration of the school and his idiot colleagues who, out of sheer jealousy, fail to acknowledge the profound lessons of his most recently published book, which the class will all be required to buy for the semester, you pack up to leave the class—forever—with a newfound despair about philosophy, and the beginnings of a very bad headache.

Epictetus would like a word with the philosophy professors of the world who proceed in this way. He asks:

> Is it then for this reason that young men shall leave
> their country and their parents, to come to this
> place and hear you explain words? Shouldn't they
> instead return home with a capacity to endure, to
> be ready to help each other, free from passions,
> immune to anxiety, and prepared for the adventure
> of life in such a way that they will be able to bear
> well the things that happen and even derive honor
> from them? And how can you give them any of
> these things that you do not possess? (III.21.8–10)

Epictetus has the highest standards for philosophy. It should be true, and it should be practical. It should give us the noblest possible picture for our lives and train us in how to live them well. Philosophy is not an esoteric arena for the assiduous cultivation of presumptuous cleverness. It's not about words and labels and "isms." And least of all is it about academic credits, textbooks and tenure. It's about the soul. It's about virtue. And freedom. And happiness. It is about the best sort of achievement in life.

In the past half-century, or more, philosophy has often been treated as if it is a sort of highbrow entertainment, or at best an intellectual adornment to be displayed at cocktail parties for the amusement of sophisticated friends. Epictetus frequently had people come to him for a little philosophy out of sheer curiosity, or as a diverting novelty, not at all thinking it might contain something that, as human beings living in this world, they deeply needed. We find him speaking to some such visitors in these strong words:

> You have come to me as if you really need nothing.
> And what could you even imagine yourself to
> be without? You're rich. You have children, and
> perhaps a wife, and many slaves. Caesar knows you,
> you have many friends in Rome, you give everyone
> the treatment they deserve—you know how to pay
> back anyone who does you a favor, and how to
> repay in kind anyone who does you a wrong. What
> do you lack? Suppose I show you that you lack the
> things that are most necessary and important for
> happiness, and that until now you have looked after
> everything other than what you should, and—to
> top it all off—you don't know either what God is or

what man is, or what is good or bad. You might
even be able to put up with my pointing out your
ignorance on all these other matters, but if I then
say that you know nothing about yourself, how is it
possible that you could endure me and listen and
stay here? (II.14.18–21)

But stay they did. And they listened. Epictetus offered his visitors a
philosophical diagnosis of their problems, and a Stoic prescription
for a cure. But he knew that philosophy, at its best, requires more
than just listening and learning. It involves putting into practice
what's been learned, and making changes in our lives. We must not
only think differently. We must live differently.

Epictetus especially welcomes those of us who come to him
aware that we are in need. We are somehow searching for something more. And we are hoping that his philosophy will give us
advice we can use. He tells us:

The beginning of philosophy for anyone who enters
into it the right way, and by the proper door, is a
consciousness of his own weakness and inability
concerning necessary things. (II.11.1–2)

Philosophy, etymologically, is the love of wisdom. It is an attitude, and an activity. It's a commitment to understanding life, and
to living out that understanding. The beginning of philosophy in
anyone's experience is a humble recognition that something is
lacking in our capacity to deal with "the necessary things" in life.
We might be very capable and quite active when it comes to desir-
able things. And we certainly seem to devote too much of our time
to apparently urgent things—the often trivial but irritatingly time
sensitive demands of daily business and hourly living. But Epictetus
believes we have "a weakness and incapacity about necessary
things" whose identification and acknowledgment can open the
door of real philosophy for us.

What are these necessary things? The difficulties we inevitably
face as we make our way in the world—disappointment, heart-
break, illness, tragedy, and the inevitable approach of death. How
do we handle these things? Epictetus believes that only philosophy
can show us the proper way to endure the negative aspects of
experience in this world. But it's not only negative things that he

means to say we lack a capacity to handle properly. We also have a weakness and incapacity concerning such necessities for human fulfillment as a sense of contentment, a stable feeling of satisfaction, and a reliable experience of happiness within whatever context surrounds us. That is why we don't feel fulfilled or complete. In our most reflective moments, we sense some sort of emptiness or need. And it is this sense that opens the door for philosophy.

Well then, what exactly is philosophy in Epictetus's view, and what does it promise to do for those of us who have recognized we do genuinely have a need? Our guide to happiness believes that philosophy is medicine for the soul. A philosopher is indeed like a physician of the spirit, and his goal is to restore us to proper health. But to do this, he may have to work hard to excise some of our diseased beliefs and values. He may have to cut away attitudes and activities that harm us. Epictetus observes at one point:

> The philosopher's school, gentlemen, is a surgery.
> You shouldn't leave it in pleasure, but in pain.
> (III.23.30)

It's not always pleasant to recognize that we have been thinking and feeling in ways that are inappropriate, or that we have been valuing and pursuing the wrong things. The good philosopher issues a wake up call that may initially be jarring to hear. It may even hurt at first to move our lives in the direction he prescribes. But the prognosis for successful treatment is very positive. It is freedom from anxiety, a new path of personal power, and true, sustainable happiness that philosophy can bring.

Epictetus wants to make it clear that in promising happiness, the philosopher is not promising us that he will give us a formula guaranteed to surround us with all the money, power, fame, status, and material toys that people typically crave in their quest to be happy. He explains that:

> Philosophy does not propose that it can secure for
> a man any external thing. (I.15.2)

The proposal is very different from that. You could say that the philosopher's specialty is internal medicine for the soul. The quest of philosophy is, according to Epictetus, first and foremost one of inner achievement. Its goal is a mindset, a perspective, a cluster of beliefs, values, attitudes, and feelings that can allow us to flourish regardless of what the external world throws in our path. This inner achievement is the best foundation there is for outer success, but it is, in itself, where Epictetus wants to focus his thought.

In one conversation, our philosopher mentions many of the frightening things in life over which we have no control, such as fevers, shipwrecks, earthquakes, lightning, unrequited love, sorrow, and envy—all of them things from which no other human being can ever completely protect us, and says:

> But the doctrine of philosophers promises to give us security and peace in even these troubles. And what does it say? If you will listen to me, wherever you are, and whatever you are doing, you will not feel suffering, or anger, or compulsion, or hindrance, but you will pass your time without worries and free from disturbance. (III.13.11)

This insightful Stoic thinker, a man of inner substance who knew how to keep his head when so many around him were both figuratively and literally losing theirs, believed that we have all been created to flourish and experience real happiness regardless of those things in life over which we have no ultimate control. It's the job of philosophy to free us from any obstacles or impediments to that purpose for which we are here.

We often live amid our pressures and stresses the way that fish swim in the sea. We're carried along by currents not of our own making, and rarely think about how we might break free of our worries while still accomplishing our proper tasks in this world. When we do come to a point of seeking something more, we should be prepared for a likely reaction on the part of at least some of those around us who are still caught in the undertow. Epictetus predicts:

> If you take an interest in philosophy, prepare yourself from the beginning to be ridiculed. Expect many to sneer at you and say, "He has suddenly returned to us as a philosopher! And where does he get this superior look?" But hold on to the things that seem to you best, as one appointed by God to this position. And remember that if you really live

these philosophical principles, the people who first
ridiculed you will later admire you. But if you let
yourself be influenced by them, you will bring on
yourself double ridicule. (E.22)

Some of the prescriptions of philosophy can at first sound strange
to those who have not yet become convinced of their own need
for something more. The attitude of the hardcore Stoic, like
Epictetus, is quite different from that of the average person. Some
aspects of his art of living may at first sound a bit strange. But in
the end, its overall, masterful power can be discerned by anyone
who pays attention. At one point, Epictetus remarks:

And so, in every activity, it's absolutely necessary
that someone who has skill is the superior over
anyone who has not. Whoever then generally
possesses the science of life, what else must he be
but a true master? (IV.1.118)

What is this science of life? And how does it contribute toward the
attitudes and perspectives that would bring us greater inner power
and personal peace, day to day? To understand it fully, we should
first look at the way in which the Stoic philosophy of Epictetus
diagnoses our needs. This former slave encourages each of us with
the suggestion to

Be seen around a philosopher's doors. You will not
disgrace yourself by being spotted there, and you
will not leave empty handed or without profit—if
you go to the philosopher as you ought. (IV.1.177)

Not every professor of philosophy can do the job. But if we
approach the right sort of philosopher, the genuinely wise practical thinker who is intent on helping us live better lives, we will
benefit greatly. So let us approach the door of Epictetus's Wisdom
Hut together and see what he has for us there.

12

OUR BIGGEST MISTAKE

We make a lot of mistakes in our lives. That's just the human condition. Fortunately, most of the mistakes we make end up being no more than minor detours on life's journey. We set the wrong goals, or take a wrong turn, learn our lesson, and then make the changes necessary to get back on track. But Epictetus thinks the biggest mistake we all make is one that keeps us from attaining the happiness we both want and deserve throughout our lives. It's one that we often do not recover from at all, unless a message as powerful as Stoic philosophy crosses our path and gets our attention.

Epictetus agrees with Aristotle that all human beings seek happiness. But he sees this as more than a quest. He thinks of it as akin to combat. We win some battles in life and lose others. Because of that, he believes it's especially important for us both to build on our successes, as battles won, and also to learn from our failures, as educational experiences that are merely temporary set-backs, since they often can teach us more than our apparent victories in preparation for further skirmishes we are yet to face.

The philosopher addresses any of us who have pursued dreams and set goals in our quest for success and happiness, and in these words urges us to review and learn from all our experiences, including the bad ones we would prefer to forget:

> Consider all the goals you've ever set for yourself,
> which you have attained, and which you have not.
> Think about how pleased you are with the successes,
> and how pained about the failures. If it's possible,
> remember the precise ways you failed. We should
> not recoil when we are engaged in the greatest
> combat, but rather take the blows that come. For

> this fight of our lives . . . is a battle for nothing less
> than good fortune and happiness. (III.25.1–3)

We are struggling throughout life to attain the results of good
fortune and happiness. But in this battle, we sadly tend to base all
our strategy on one big mistake. We live it each day. It's an assumption that underlies our thoughts, reactions, emotions, attitudes, and
actions. It determines how we fight for happiness, how we react to
success, and how we are affected by setbacks.

The symptoms that we are somehow approaching life wrong
are numerous. We feel stress, anxiety, worry, pressure, and exhaus-
tion in our daily lives. We find hope tangled up with dread. We
somehow deep down fear the worst. We feel squeezed from all
directions, and by a great many forces. But Epictetus has both surprising and comforting news for us. He urges:

> Remember this general truth, that it is we who
> squeeze ourselves, who put ourselves in difficulties.
> And, actually, it is our opinions that squeeze us and
> limit us. (I.25.28)

It is, he proclaims, not the external forces in our lives, but our own
beliefs about those forces that pressure us and bring on us all the
negative experience that has become so characteristic of modern
life. In another discourse, he remarks:

> Nothing else is the cause of anxiety or loss of
> tranquility except our own opinion. (III.19.3)

In yet another conversation, he says to a person of great wealth:

> You have utensils of gold, but your opinions,
> your beliefs, your pursuits, your desires, are of
> earthenware. (III.9.18–19)

Our opinions, our beliefs, our pursuits, and our customary desires
are almost all based on the one big mistake Epictetus thinks we
habitually and perpetually make. He comments about most of the
people around him:

> They want the things that lead to happiness, but
> they look for them in the wrong place. (III.23.34–35)

Our big mistake consists in looking for happiness in the wrong place.

> The condition and characteristic of an unenlightened person is this: he never expects from himself profit or harm, but from externals. The condition and characteristic of the philosopher is this: he expects all advantage and all harm from himself. (E.48)

What is this big mistake we all make? Our biggest mistake in life is the way in which we look to the external world for our happiness. We think that external things will bring us lasting good or ill, personal profit or harm. But it is only internal things that ultimately can do that. Epictetus wants to help us correct our big mistake and refocus our lives on those internal matters of the soul, those matters of the will and of virtue over which we do have control. True success and true happiness come from refocusing ourselves within. He counsels:

> Remember this general rule and you will need no other advice. But if you desperately seek external things, you must of necessity ramble up and down in obedience to the will of a master. And who is this master? Anyone who has the power over those things you seek to gain or to avoid. (II.2.25–26)

Epictetus believes that our big mistake has a number of unfortunate consequences. First, it tends to enslave us to other people. If we crave more and more money, we are beholden to those people around us who already have it, and thus have the power to give or withhold it. When we crave any external thing, like power, or luxury, or status, we position ourselves to be tempted to unworthy, obsequious flattery, or other forms of inauthentic action, in subjugation to those who seem to control the objects we desire. Our philosopher puts his general point in a strikingly absolute way when he says:

> Remember that it's not only a desire for power and wealth that can make us low and subject to others, but even a craving for quiet, leisure, travel abroad, and a good education. For to speak plainly,

whatever the external thing may be, any positive
value that we give it places us in subjection to others.
(IV.4.1)

If you want something that only someone else can give, or that
someone else can prevent, you are dependent on that person. If
you want to avoid something that is within the power of another
person to unleash or restrain, then again you are in the power of
that person. So externals can subjugate—if we let them. Epictetus
believes that inner subjugation to any other man or woman is a
state of being that is completely without honor.

A second point made by our philosopher of inner strength is
that externals can demoralize. If we depend for our happiness on
anything outside our control, we set ourselves up for such negative
emotional states as worry, fear, resentment, envy, and disappointment. Epictetus observes:

When I see a man anxious, I ask, "What does he
want?" If he did not want something that isn't in
his power, how could he be anxious? For this very
reason, a lute player singing by himself has no
anxiety, but when he enters the theater, he gets
anxious even if he has a good voice and plays the
lute well. The problem is that he not only wants
to sing well, but also to obtain applause. But this is
not in his power. Accordingly, where he has skill,
there he has confidence. (II.13.1–3)

There is a fine point here. Epictetus says it is not within the power
of a musician to obtain applause. But this can seem plainly wrong.
How can he say this? What does he mean? Many musicians obtain
vigorous applause whenever they perform. And certainly it is
because of their performance. Doesn't it follow that the applause
was indeed within their power to elicit? The power to attain excellence in the performance can seem to be exactly the same as the
power to obtain applause for that performance.

Epictetus wants us to think a bit more carefully. The musician
can exercise his power to perform well in the privacy of his own
home and elicit no applause as a result, because there is no crowd.
For applause to occur as a result of his performance, there obvi-
ously must be a crowd. And this is an external circumstance over

which many excellent musicians have little or no control. Early in his career, a musician may not be able to get bookings into venues that will draw a crowd. He may not be able to get the right kind of publicity to attract people to his performances. But even with an audience, there is no guarantee of applause. A musician may on occasion find himself playing in front of people who dislike his instrument, and who are forced by circumstances to hear him perform when they would prefer to be doing something else, and are at that moment in no mood for listening to his music, eager to get on with other activities or to hear a more famous musician instead. He may be playing in front of people who dislike his particular kind of music, are intoxicated, or are just irritable, and he can perform with all his customary excellence, only to obtain boos and catcalls. Excellence is no guarantee of appreciative acclamation.

Some writers become bestselling authors. Others do not. And the difference is not often talent. No writer can guarantee a *New York Times* Bestseller. He has control over the quality of his content, but not the quantity of his sales. It is up to other people whether his book sells well or not. No one has the power to make a million people buy a book. No one has the power to make a single person he doesn't know buy his book. A top actor can have a huge hit today and a giant flop next year—despite his complete conviction that both movies are equally good. Some artists are successful in their own time. Others are not. Some public speakers enjoy standing ovations. Many others do not. And what is of particular interest here is that one speaker can give the same talk on two different occasions with equal energy, enthusiasm, and excellence, and see one audience go wild—standing, stomping, clapping, whistling, and shouting accolades—while the other group may respond with nothing more than very warm, polite applause.

We can never guarantee external results. Something that is not within our power may go terribly wrong. Something outside our control may end up lacking. As long as life is sufficiently complex, and people are basically free, the results we obtain in the outer world are never entirely up to us. Ironically, we often most reliably obtain the external results we'd like to see—those things over which we never have full control—when we learn to concentrate our attention on those things over which we do have control. And this is what Epictetus wants us to see.

Focusing on things and craving results that are not strictly in our power can tend to undermine our confidence in ourselves and in our lives. An unduly external orientation often keeps us from best using the power we do have in such a way as to attain the fulfillment of our true potential. The wrong focus can distract us from the inner resources we possess and divert us from the activities we need to be engaged in for the best chance of producing the results we most deeply need.

External things like money and status can come and go, but Epictetus is convinced that inner happiness is meant to be our ongoing enjoyment. He teaches:

> Examine yourself, whether you want to be rich or happy. If you want to be rich, you should know that it is neither a good thing nor at all in your power. But if you want to be happy, you should realize that it is both a good thing and in your power. Wealth is a temporary loan of Fortune, but happiness comes from the will. (F.XIX)

Why is being rich not a good thing? The value of money depends wholly on how it is used. Wealth can have good effects, or it can destroy a person. It is in itself neither good nor bad. A wish to be rich is inherently incomplete. Why do we want money? Because we think it can buy happiness, or at least push us in the right direction for happiness. But it often does not. In one discourse, the philosopher gives this rich illustration:

> Just as you wouldn't choose to sail in a large and ornately decorated, gold-laden ship if you knew it was going to sink and you would drown, don't choose to live in a big expensive house if the result there is that you will be disturbed. (F.XIV)

In a related conversation, he says:

> As it is better to lie squeezed in a narrow bed and be healthy than to be tossed with disease on a broad couch, so also it's better to contract yourself within a small competence and be happy than to have a great fortune and be miserable. (F.XXIV)

When he recommends contracting ourselves "within a small competence," Epictetus is not here to be taken as necessarily recommending the setting of only small goals in life. He is suggesting rather that the central focus of our thoughts, plans, attitudes and energies should stay close to home, to what we can control, to the small sphere of real personal competence that we do command— matters of the inner self, issues of character, concerns of personal performance, and matters of the will.

It's important not to misunderstand Epictetus here. He is not for a moment suggesting that wealth, or power, or any external condition that we often pursue is in itself a bad thing. He is just convinced that externals are not the good things we often imagine. They can function well or badly in a person's life. And how they fit into a life is ultimately determined by the core inner attitudes with which that life is lived.

Is your focus proper? Are you in control of yourself? Or have external things become your masters? Are other people charting the course of your life? Or are you true to yourself?

Putting our hopes in anything outside ourselves within this created, external world is, from Epictetus's point of view, wrong. We are meant to build our lives from within, to solidify the core, and strengthen the soul to such an extent that it can flourish within any context. He advises:

> If anyone is unhappy, remember that his
> unhappiness is his own fault. God has made all
> men to be happy, and to be free from worries.
> (III.XXIV.2)

We cannot be free from perturbations unless we break free from this big mistake of taking externals to be, in themselves, intrinsically good or intrinsically bad in our lives. In a later discourse, Epictetus reasons with a real or imaginary dialogue partner in this way:

> Does freedom seem to you good? It's the greatest
> good. Is it possible then that he who obtains
> the greatest good can be unhappy or fare badly?
> No. Whoever then you see unhappy, unfortunate,
> or complaining, you can judge with confidence
> that they are not free. (IV.1.52)

The key to happiness is freedom. Freedom from any enslavement. Freedom from our big mistake of looking to externals for our sense of self, and for our sense of what is good. We need freedom in order to be able to chart our own paths in this world. Any form of life achievement that does not allow for an inner sense of wellbeing is, according to Epictetus, fundamentally ill conceived.

Our philosopher of personal freedom declares:

> Anyone is free who lives as he wishes to live. (IV.1.1)

And then,

> No one is free who is not master of himself. (F.CXIV)

But how then is this freedom that is rooted in self-mastery, the form of liberation so prized by Epictetus, to be attained? In a passage seemingly on another topic altogether, he gives us a hint. He says:

> Time relieves the foolish from sorrow, but reason relieves the wise. (CXXVIII)

Why do we ever persist in sorrow? Why do we continue to worry or fear? What allows us to be at times emotionally unhinged by a sudden turn of events? Epictetus has a simple answer. It is only because we have not let reason lead us.

The Stoic recipe for freedom is to allow our deepest, and highest, capacity—our ability to reason—to form our innermost attitudes and thoughts. When we understand how to do this, we will be able to achieve the Stoic freedom, the inner resilience, the emotional balance, and the enduring happiness that Epictetus wants for us all. And this is the strongest possible foundation for any other sort of achievement that we might ever want to pursue.

13

STOIC FREEDOM

Epictetus understands that, whatever the topic, philosophers can go on and on, endlessly drawing distinctions, constructing arguments, and quoting each other in great detail. He knows that the whole resulting enterprise of philosophy can at times seem intellectually daunting and exceedingly complex. It's noteworthy that his sympathy over our plight in acquainting ourselves with the works of philosophers occurred many centuries before the likes of Kant, Hegel, or Heidegger would set new heights in the practice of disgorging deep and convoluted thoughts onto paper. But even in his time, our philosophical guide thought we could use some help in cutting to the chase. He reasons:

> The chief doctrine of philosophers is quite
> brief. It takes very few words to say that a human
> being's purpose is to follow the gods, and that
> the nature of good is a proper use of appearances.
> (I.20.14–15)

This may not capture the thought of just any philosopher, but it is a handy summary, once we understand it, for the teachings of the Stoic sages from whom Epictetus takes his cue.

The main Stoic conception of the universe, in the time of Epictetus, saw it as run by a benevolent intelligence, a rational providence ultimately productive of good. God was conceived of, or alternatively, at times, "the gods" were viewed as, paradigmatically free, happy, and virtuous, a best possible exemplar for human emulation. For a Stoic, "following the gods" would mean acting as a free being, developing inner virtue and accepting the course of external events in this world as, in one way or

another, the outworking of divine providence, and thus, ultimately, as good.

For a philosopher like Epictetus to say that "the nature of the
good is a proper use of appearances" is an articulation in brief of
the whole Stoic stance on life. It will help us at our current stage
to get clear on what this means.

The Stoics followed Plato in distinguishing carefully between
appearances and realities. Things do not often appear to us as they
really are. Or, to put it in common parlance, appearances can be
deceiving. Plato and Epictetus, along with many other philosophers, believed that most people live their lives enslaved by
appearances, captivated by illusions, and thus out of touch with
true reality.

What Epictetus called "appearances" are unavoidable. It is up to
the wise person to use them well. We are to be discerning, following accurate appearances to the truth, and resisting the lure of false
appearances that threaten to lead us astray. Epictetus asserts that:

> The business of the wise and good man is to use
> appearances in conformity to nature. And just as it
> is the nature of every soul to assent to the truth, to
> dissent from the false, and to remain open when
> something is uncertain, so it is also its nature to be
> moved toward a desire of the good, to an aversion
> from the bad, and concerning that which is neither
> good nor bad, it feels indifferent. (III.3.1–2)

The wise person avoids falsehood and embraces truth, while desir-
ing good, shunning bad, and remaining fundamentally indifferent
about what has no intrinsic value. The Stoic insight is that most of
life's problems come from violating this simple formula. We too
often believe the wrong things, pursue the wrong things, and get
all worked up about the wrong things. The essence of Stoic freedom is to escape these errors and bring the right attitudes to life.

Epictetus lays out a major philosophical claim made by Stoic
thinkers when he says:

> Some things are good, some are bad, and others
> are indifferent. The good things are the virtues and
> things that partake of virtues, the bad things are
> the vices and things that partake of them, and the

> indifferent things are all those items that lie between
> the virtues and the vices: wealth, health, life, death,
> pleasure, and pain. (II.19.13)

Notice something striking and surprising here for a modern sensibility. The only things that are deemed good without qualification are inner matters of the soul, or the will—matters of virtue, or the intentions and choices productive of virtue. Likewise, nothing is bad without qualification except again inner states of the soul having to do with vice. The vast territory of what Epictetus calls "the indifferent" encompasses all matters of the external world, and even the states of our bodies and bodily sensations. All this is considered external to the will, and thus of no intrinsic value, either positive or negative. And yet many of these items are precisely the things—wealth, power, social status, attractiveness, pleasure, and luxury—that are craved as the apparatus of happiness in any materialistic society, ancient or modern.

We get a further clarification in this statement:

> The nature of the good is a certain kind of will.
> The nature of the bad is a certain kind of will. What
> then are external things? They are materials for
> the will, which it can use for its own good or evil.
> (I.29.1–2)

The will—the fundamental human power of choice—is characterized by Epictetus as the seat and source of all value in human life. Nothing is intrinsically good or bad but a person's will, and modifications or actions of a will. Everything else is either of instrumental value only, depending on how it is used by the will, or else of no value at all.

The Roman poet Terence once claimed that, "Wealth is a blessing to those who know how to use it, a curse to those who don't." And this is true of any external thing. Power can be used well or badly. So can material objects. The same is true of physical attractiveness. The whole of the external world, Stoic philosophy tells us, is just a warehouse of materials for the will. We should never get too excited or upset over external things. They are in themselves neither intrinsically good nor inherently bad. Only what we choose to do regarding them has that status.

This sets us up for the main Stoic advice concerning the attainment of personal freedom that we all need for a secure experience of happiness in this life. We must take up the right attitude and actions with respect to things in the world:

> In life, the chief business is to distinguish and separate things and say, "Externals are not in my power. My inner will is in my power. Where then will I look for good and bad? Within, in the things of my own." But among those things that don't belong to you, call nothing good, or bad, or profit, or damage, or anything of the kind. (II.5.4–5)

There are two categories of things in this world: things we can control and things we cannot control. We should be concerned about the things we can control, and not about the things we can't control. This is a central piece of Stoic advice that has reverberated down through the ages.

Epictetus makes the following point about the wise person's inner equilibrium and freedom:

> When you have learned not to esteem things that are external and independent of the will, but have realized that these things only are your own: to exercise judgment well, to form beliefs, to move toward an object, to desire, or to turn away from a thing—then where will there be any room for flattery or inferiority? (III.24.56)

When we recognize that only three things are really in our power: assent, aspiration, and action—what we believe, what we desire, and what we move toward—we free ourselves radically from those attitudes of subservience and emotional bondage that hold too many people back from their proper development and inner personal success in this world. We then can stand tall in the personal integrity that is so hard to find in this life.

Recognizing the intrinsic value of our inner states and the lack of intrinsic value to be found in externals leads to Stoic freedom and dignity. Epictetus believes that it also leads to happiness. Snippets of two conversations indicate this. First, he remarks concerning the will that:

It is through this that we are unfortunate, or that
we are fortunate, that we blame one another, or are
pleased with one another. In a word, it is this that,
if we neglect it, makes for unhappiness, but, if we
carefully look after it, makes for happiness. (II.23.29)

Secondly, Epictetus teaches:

There is only one way to happiness, and so one
rule to use from morning until night. That rule is:
Don't be concerned about things that are outside the
power of your will, and don't believe that anything
external is really yours, but give up all that to God.
(IV.4.39)

Here we find the two great Stoic themes intertwined: We should
concentrate our attention on inner matters of the will, as the only
true path to human flourishing and happiness, and each day we
should take up a fundamental attitude of creaturely release—of giving up all external things to God. What is within our power is our
concern. All else is God's business.

In a longer passage, we see again these themes:

Being by nature noble, great of soul, and free, the
rational man sees that of all the things around him,
some are free from hindrance and within his power,
and some are subject to hindrance and lie in the
power of others. He recognizes that the things free
from external hindrance are in the power of his
will, and that those subject to hindrance are not in
the power of his will. For this reason, if he thinks
that his good and his interest lie only in those things
that are free from hindrance and within his own
power, he will be free, prosperous, happy, safe from
harm, magnanimous, pious, thankful to God for
everything, and will not find fault with any things
that are not in his power, or assign blame for any
of them. But if anyone thinks that his good and his
interest are in externals and things not in the
power of his will, he will inevitably be hindered and
blocked, and will end up in servitude to those who

> do have some control over what he desires and
> fears. Such a person will certainly also be impious,
> because he will think that he is at times harmed by
> God, and he will be unjust, because he will always
> claim more than what properly belongs to him.
> All that will make him miserable and inferior.
> (IV.7.8–11)

Notice also this passage in which Epictetus explicitly connects our proper attitude toward divinity with what we can call "The Principle of the Will":

> As to piety toward the gods, you should know
> that this is the main thing: to have true beliefs
> about them, to think that they exist, and that they
> administer everything justly and well, and to fix
> yourself in this principle—to obey them, and yield
> to them in everything that happens, freely accepting
> it as being accomplished by the wisest intelligence.
> If you live like this, you will never blame the gods
> for anything, or ever accuse them of neglecting
> you. This important result can't be accomplished
> in any other way than by withdrawing from the
> things that are not in our power, and recognizing
> good and evil only in those things that are within
> our power. (E.31)

You might even call this The Piety Argument for The Principle of the Will. Epictetus is arguing that the only proper attitude toward providence is to accept whatever happens in the external world as being in some sense God's will, if not to effect, then at least to allow. When, at some emotional level, we accept externals and give them over to God, we free ourselves to concentrate on what is within our power, and what is our primary job in this life—to work on inner matters of the soul and will.

It doesn't matter whether you're rich or poor, a C.E.O. or a custodian—your primary job is always personal growth in virtue. You are here to bring the right attitudes and actions to the people around you and to the external world. But it is always the inner you that is your first workplace and most important task.

Epictetus thinks it is the inner attitude of Stoic acceptance that will give each of us the greatest dignity in life. He maintains:

> Anyone who is dissatisfied with the present and what is given by Fortune is an ignorant man in life. But the person who bears all things nobly and rationally, as well as anything that proceeds from them, is worthy of being considered a man.
> (F.CXXXV)

This is what our philosopher gives us as his conception of a full and complete human life. It is a life of freedom, happiness, acceptance, and dignity. It is a life imbued with inner resilience.

The philosopher of freedom wants to convince us that our bodies are just jars of clay, sacks of sand, or bags of bones. We ourselves are souls. Each of us is a will, a center of choosing, and a self that is capable of cultivating virtue. No reductionist philosophy or misapplied science can ever demonstrate otherwise. Whatever the role of our bodies might be in supporting the reality of our minds, it is the mental sphere, the inner spiritual activity of attitude and choice, that is definitive of who we finally are and what we ultimately can do.

The things that matter intrinsically are inner states of the will. Sometimes, Epictetus seems to say that externals are hardly worthy of our attention at all. We should not get too excited about them or too discouraged. They are firmly within the category of "the indifferent." And yet commentators on Stoicism have often pointed out that a reasonable version of the Stoic view need not deny altogether the value of things in the external world. Despite the connotations often associated with Stoicism in common parlance, Stoics don't even have to maintain that we should never be moved emotionally by things external to us. In one passage, Epictetus himself avers:

> He is wise who doesn't grieve for the things he doesn't have, but rejoices for the things he does have. (F.CXXIX)

Certainly, a person who "rejoices" over what he has is not being totally unmoved by things in the external world. He is not failing to attach any value whatsoever to externals. And he is experiencing a very positive emotion. We can read Epictetus loosely as holding that externals do not have intrinsic value in and of themselves, but that this is compatible with their having extrinsic, or instrumental, value in our lives, depending on how we use them—which brings us back again to the choices of the will as the ultimate fount of value in the world.

It is hard to see how any rational, sensitive human being could assign externals no value whatsoever. But we can still appreciate Epictetus's point that we tend to invest ourselves far too deeply in the vicissitudes of the external world, when we should be building our own characters first and foremost instead. Stoic freedom from placing too much value on externals is a freedom to develop and achieve in a way that allows you to remain true to yourself.

Epictetus sees the search for such freedom as the ultimate point of philosophy. He says:

> Give me one young man who has come to the school of philosophy with this intention, who is a real champion for this matter and will say, "I relinquish everything else—it is enough for me if it will ever be in my power to live unencumbered by hindrance and trouble, to experience all things like a free man, and to look up to heaven as a friend of God, and fear nothing that can happen." Let anyone point out such a man to me and I will say, "Come, young man, into the possession of what is properly yours, for it is your destiny to adorn philosophy. These possessions, these books, and these discourses belong to you." (II.17.29–30)

This, according to Epictetus, is the Stoic ideal.

14

OBSTACLES AND ANGER

Appearances can be as important as realities. In particular, how we handle appearances can be as crucial as how we handle the objective realities that underlie them. Our interpretations of situations, and our responses to them, can end up being much more important than the situations themselves. That's why the Stoics are so concerned about emotion, attitude, and perspective.

How do we handle what life throws at us? Are we empowered or unhinged as we deal with the things that cross our paths? Two people can be in exactly the same objective situation. One blows up and the other remains calm. Who is likelier to have the most perceptive judgment and make the best decisions in that situation? The Stoics are convinced that only our own inner strength, and the use that we make of appearances, will move us forward productively in the world.

Epictetus recognizes that there are three basic ways in which we can deal with unexpected and unwanted developments in our experience. The first possible response, the one dominant in the lives of those who have not attained Stoic freedom, is anger. When something happens that we don't like, we tend to respond with some version and degree of that negative emotion broadly known as anger. We react with irritation, frustration, inner hostility, or manifest rage. All the great Stoic philosophers viewed anger as one of the most self-defeating and even self-destructive of inner states to be in. Balled up in our own negative emotions, we often cannot think, feel, or act as we should.

The second possible response to an unpleasant surprise is to take action. When something happens that is unwanted, and we are in a position to do something about it, we should let our sense of right and wrong motivate us to take any reasonable initiative necessary to correct the situation. The Stoic advice is that we should use our reason to assess what we confront, as well as the possible paths of action we might take, and then allow reason to guide any active response that is both prudent and likely to be effective.

But action is not always either possible, or prudent, or even remotely likely to be effective. So the third response we can make to any unwanted turn of events is to take up a fundamental inner attitude of acceptance. This is the inner state recommendation for which Stoicism is most noted. But it's the Stoic's main concern to urge us to choose either action or acceptance over the negative response of anger. And it is the opposite course that most people are tempted to take most of the time.

Epictetus is offering us a program of reform for the ways in which we react to things in the world, as well as for the initiatives that we ourselves launch. He reminds us of the starting point for a Stoic life stance with the words:

> To what should I pay attention? First to some general insights I am always ready to use, principles so important I won't even sleep without them, or get up in the morning, or drink, or eat, or to speak to another person without them: No one is the master of anyone else's will. And in the will alone, good and bad exist. So no other person has the power either to bring me good or to force me into evil—I alone have power over myself in this regard. When I get these ideas straight, why should I ever be disturbed about external things? (IV.12.7–9)

But most of us are frequently disturbed about external things. It has surprised me, as a philosopher, to learn how pervasive the particular form of disturbance generally known as anger is in the modern world. It undermines marriages, tears apart friendships, wrecks business relationships, and sabotages lives. It prevents positive achievement. It polarizes politicians, and it perpetuates cycles of violence and recrimination around the world. Because of the power and pervasiveness of this one negative inner state— the emotional disturbance of anger—the Stoic philosophers comment on it a great deal. Epictetus in particular offers us some practical and effective ways of loosening the hold it often has in our lives.

First, in many conversations, the philosopher offers us a mental technique of contextualizing, or putting everything into its proper perspective. One example finds him saying:

> What then, must I be brought to trial? Must someone I know have a fever, another go out on a dangerous voyage, someone else die, another be condemned? Yes, these things happen, for it is impossible in such a physical body, in such a universe of things, among so many living together, that such events should not ever happen, some to one, and others to others.
> (II.5.27)

In a large and complex universe, matters will sometimes go awry, things will bump into each other, and events will intersect in occasionally unfortunate ways. But when something does happen that seems bad, our philosopher urges that if we put it into this larger cosmic perspective, it will not shock and dismay us so much.

Whenever we are unhinged by a turn of events, it is because we are viewing those events in a very constricted context, from an unduly narrow perspective. In a small setting, anything can look big. But when we mentally step back and set the event disturbing us into a larger and broader contextualization, gaining a bigger picture perspective on it, we find that it will not look either as surprising or as big and important. In the grandest scheme of things, our most dreaded obstacles take on a different and much less imposing look. According to the Stoics, it is the task of reason to give us this contextualization.

I have come to believe that imagination guided by reason is of the utmost importance in helping us with any emotionally effective contextualization exercise. It is often the imagination out of control that is responsible for emotion out of control. And while we should govern imagination by reason, it is only the power of the imagination that is able to tame emotion. The Stoics are right to say that reason must lead the way. But without deploying the power of the imagination, it is unlikely that reason will ever prevail, either in the realm of emotion or in the realm of action.

Epictetus thinks that one of the most important things in life is how we "manage appearances." By this, he means not how we manage the image we project to other people, our own appearance in the world, but rather how we interpret the appearances by which other things in the external world present themselves to us. We have little control over what might appear around the next bend of the road we are traveling, but we have immense control over what we do with those appearances as they come to us. We need to learn to manage, or properly govern, our interpretation of appearances. That will allow us to manage, or govern, in turn, our emotions and actions in response to those appearances. In one place, Epictetus says:

> Right away then practice saying to every harsh appearance: "You are merely an appearance, and in no way what you appear to be." Then examine it by the rules you possess, and by this first and chiefly: ask whether it relates to the things that are in your power, or to the things that are not in your power. And if it relates to anything not in your power, be ready to say that it does not concern you. (E.I)

This is, in effect, a second form of contextualizing, or changing our perspective. In addition to imaginatively putting something unpleasant into a bigger picture context, we are to ask ourselves which of two possible categories it falls into: the category of things within our power, or the category of things that are beyond our power. A contextualization that puts anything into the latter category is sufficient to deflect the concern of any wise person, Epictetus urges us to understand.

Our philosopher does touch on the topic of imagination when he discusses our mental ability to "draw lively pictures" for ourselves. The second psychological technique he suggests for dealing with irritating or angering circumstances is one of quieting the mind, and then the tongue, by utilizing this ability we have for drawing lively pictures. When something happens that might naturally elicit a reaction of anger, Epictetus would have you take a mental break. Draw a deep breath, go blank, and then use your imagination in a calming way: Picture a peaceful, placid scene, such as a beautiful beach on a sunny day, or a bright and lush garden, with leaves rustling in a gentle breeze. Project yourself there mentally, if only for a few seconds, to allow your blood pressure to return to normal, your heart rate to calm, and your emotions to settle before you speak, react, or decide any course of action to take.

Whenever a difficult or harsh appearance presents itself to us, Epictetus advises the following:

> In the first place, don't be rushed to judgment by the
> rapidity of the appearance, but say, "Appearances,
> wait for me a little. Let me see who you are and what
> you're really all about. Let me put you to the test."
> And then do not allow the appearance to lead you on
> and draw for you lively pictures of what will follow.
> If you let it, it will carry you off where it pleases. But
> rather bring in to counter it some other beautiful
> and noble appearance that can neutralize it. And if
> you are accustomed to doing this, you will see what
> shoulders, what muscles, what strength you have.
> (II.18.24-26)

In addition to using reason and imagination to accomplish both contextualization and the taking of mental refreshment breaks, Epictetus's remarks here also encourage a third use of the mind, this time a specific act of restraining and redirecting the imagination. He insists that we not allow any untoward external events, or their appearances, to lead our imaginations on in negative and unhelpful ways.

Think about any instance of someone's doing something that makes you mad. Most often, you immediately let your imagination loose to be led away by appearances. You mentally envision the person who has hurt or upset you engaging in those actions. You may even 'see' yourself taking revenge. If you allow your imagination to move in such directions, you give up control of your own emotions to the power of those appearances that first struck you. Epictetus advises a refusal to indulge your imagination in this way. When you catch yourself imagining the wrongdoer committing his heinous deed, stop yourself right there. Refuse to go forward into this realm of mental picturing. When you find yourself imagining any possibly terrible consequences of something that has just happened, stop again. The imagination inflames the emotions and can feed the negative states of irritation, frustration, anger and even despair.

So, in summary, Epictetus offers us a bundle of techniques for freeing ourselves from the main negative emotional state that tends to hold us back in this life, the state of anger in any of its forms. In response to whatever happens to upset you, he urges:

(1) Put it in perspective,

(2) Take a Mental Break,

(3) Refresh your spirit,

(4) Control your imagination.

Our wise advisor believes that such techniques will help us in any specific circumstances to react better to disappointment, and that they will also begin to cultivate in us habits of response that are much healthier and more productive than the habits of anger and resentment we too often have.

Epictetus generally seems to view habit, tendency, or disposition, as very important in human life. A few passages on this will begin to reveal some of his perspectives on the long-term issue of virtue in daily living. First, he says, quite generally:

> Every habit and ability is maintained and increased by the corresponding actions: the habit of walking is maintained by walking, the habit of running by running. If you want to be a good reader, then read. If you want to be a writer, write. But when you have not read for thirty days in a row, but have done something else instead, you will know the result. In the same way, if you have been lying in bed for ten days, get up and try to take a long walk, and you will see how your legs have been weakened. Generally, if you want to make anything a habit, do it; if you don't want to make it a habit, or want to get rid of a habit, don't do it, but accustom yourself to doing something else in its place.
>
> It's the same way with the emotions in your soul. When you have been angry, you need to realize that not only has this one evil befallen you, but that you have also increased the habit of responding like this and experiencing anger again. You've really thrown fuel on the fire. (II.18.1–5)

Later he continues, applying this insight to the tendency that we all have toward a response of anger in unwanted circumstances:

> If you don't want to be an angry person, don't feed the habit. Throw nothing on it that will increase it.

> At first, just try to keep calm and quiet, and count the days on which you have not been angry. I used to experience this passion every day, then every other day, and after a while, every third day, then every fourth or so. Once you have gone for thirty days without feeling it, make a sacrifice to God. For the habit at first begins to be weakened, and then eventually is completely destroyed. (II.18.12–13)

A change of habit is never instantaneous. It always takes time. Epictetus here presents thirty days as the amount of time it takes to eradicate a habit of reacting with anger. The eradication of the habit does not itself guarantee that you will never thereafter again feel anger; it just means that you will not have a firm tendency or disposition inclining you to respond in this way. The best avoidance of anger will depend on the cultivation of a different habit or tendency of response, such as a tendency to calm yourself, put things into perspective, refresh your spirit, and then take deliberative action in whatever manner is appropriate.

Epictetus would have us attend carefully to how we react to both external events and other people. The Stoic freedom that he prizes depends on taking a certain inner stance and vigilantly directing our attention to whatever is most important about a situation, in so far as it touches on our primary duty to cultivate our inner virtues. A lapse of attention can allow old habits to reassert themselves, and create for us problems once more. He says:

> When you have relaxed your attention for a short time, don't imagine you can easily recover it whenever you choose. Let this thought be present to you, that as a result of the fault committed today, your affairs will of necessity be in worse shape in the future. First, and this is what causes the most trouble, a habit of not attending is in this way formed in you, then a habit of deferring your attention. And this is how from time to time you get accustomed to putting off the happy life, the experience of living and being in harmony with nature. If this sort of procrastination of attention were beneficial, a complete omission of attention would likely be even better. But if it is not at all

> beneficial, then why not maintain your attention
> constantly? "Today I choose to play." Well, then,
> shouldn't you play with attention? "I choose to
> sing." What then hinders you from doing so with
> attention? Is there any part of life this doesn't apply
> to, anything at all to which attention should not
> extend? (IV.12.1–4)

The subject of attention, as we have noted earlier, is one shared by Eastern and Western philosophy, as well as by all the world's great religious traditions. What we attend to, and how we attend to it, will determine how we think, how we feel, and how we act. Epictetus insists that we not sleep walk through life, but live attending to our experience in all the right ways. When we do as he advises, we can use appearances appropriately and retain our equilibrium even if tremendous difficulties cross our path.

15

A GOOD LIFE AND DEATH

Too many of us are more concerned about what other people think of us than about what kind of people we really are. And this can skew our approach to the ethics of personal achievement, as well as of life generally. When image displaces character as our primary focus, we become more concerned about cultivating what the people around us happen to approve rather than what is right in itself. Epictetus, not one to mince words, pointedly asks:

> Do you want to do good or to be praised? (II.23.7)

His advice in this regard is vivid. He says:

> The sun doesn't wait for prayers and incantations
> to persuade it to rise, but immediately shines and is
> saluted by all. In the same way, you shouldn't wait
> for a clapping of hands, shouts, and praise before
> you do good, but rather be a doer of good voluntarily,
> and you will be loved like the sun. (F.LXXXVIII)

It's an apparently widespread human tendency to live reactively. In modern terms, Epictetus wants us to be proactive. He urges us to take the initiative to do good in the world. Don't wait until the right thing is popular; do it now. That is his insistence.

But how can we become reliable doers of good? By becoming inwardly good. For Epictetus, the ethics of everyday life is fundamentally a matter of cultivating the will. As he understands it, the will is not only our faculty of choosing—the ability to decide and enact our decisions—it is the seat of virtue or vice, determining the quality of choices that will be made. He says:

When the will has been set right, a man who
was not good becomes good, but when it fails, he
becomes bad. (II.23.28)

How then do we set the will right? The answer is actually quite simple. First, we should learn, remember, and practice the principles
of Stoic freedom, breaking the bonds that otherwise chain our wills
to an inappropriate fixation on and pursuit of external things. We
should use the power of reason we all have to govern our emotions and choices appropriately. We should subject our imaginations to the direction of reason as well. And we should do everything within our power to associate with people whose company
will improve us in both wisdom and virtue.

Epictetus, with his standard vividness of expression, says:

If a man has frequent interaction with others either
for talk, or drinking together, or generally for social
purposes, he must either become like them, or
change them to be like him. For if anyone places a
piece of cold, damp charcoal up against a piece that
is burning, either the quenched charcoal will put out
the other, or the burning charcoal will eventually
light that which was quenched. Since the danger is
so great, we should enter into such intimacies with
those of a common sort only with great caution. And
remember that it's impossible for a man to keep
company with someone covered with soot without
getting some of that soot on himself. (III.16.1–4)

This is indeed a vivid image. Soot travels, clings, and stains. Dirt is
contagious. Clean takes work. In another common metaphor, if you
lie down with dogs, you'll likely get up with fleas. As great philosophers always have seen, and as our folk wisdom long has acknowledged, behavior can indeed be a very contagious thing.

Epictetus addresses those students who have come to study
with him for the purpose of developing wisdom and virtue and
adds:

Until good thoughts and habits of mind are firmly
fixed in you and you've acquired a certain power
for your security, I advise you to be careful in your

> association with common, coarse people. If you are
> not, then every day, like wax in the sun, whatever
> you have inscribed in your minds at school will be
> melted away. Stay out of this heat as long as your
> thoughts are waxen. (III.16.9)

We become like the people we're around. Therefore, we should
spend as much time as we can with the wise and good.

Epictetus sees us as essentially social beings. Thus our socializing has great significance for who we are and what we become. We should always remember that people are vastly more valuable than things. Material possessions can be convenient, comforting, and enjoyable. They can even be life saving. There is nothing wrong with having nice things. But having good friends is much more important. The sage recommends:

> Instead of a herd of oxen, endeavor to assemble
> herds of friends in your house. (F.LXVII)

It's a lot less messy, and much more fulfilling.

Who then should we have as friends? The good. The wise. The free. But how are these people to be recognized? What is the proper way for choosing associates? Human beings use all sorts of principles of selection. We hang out with others of similar background. Or we gravitate toward people with common interests. Epictetus has a philosophical test for friendship. He says:

> Don't examine what most men care about—whether
> others were born of the same parents, share the
> same background, or studied with the same
> teacher—but ask this only: Where do they place
> their interest, in external things or the will? If all
> they care about is externals, then don't consider
> them friends. Don't think them trustworthy, constant, brave or free. Don't even regard them as men,
> if you have any judgment. (II.22.26–27)

He goes on:

> But if you hear that, in truth, these men think that
> good is to be found only where the will is, and

> where there is right use of appearances, then no
> longer trouble yourself about whether they are
> father or son, or brothers, or have associated a
> long time and are companions, but when you have
> learned this only, you can declare with confidence
> that they are friends, as you can consider them to
> be faithful and just. For where else is friendship
> than where there is fidelity and modesty, where
> there is a communion of honest things and of
> nothing else? (II.22.29–30)

Of course, this is just a presentation of the basic Stoic worldview and stance as the requirement for true friendship.

The philosopher then imagines an objection to his strict criterion of friendship. What if someone has been my companion or associate for a long time and often has shown me good will or even affection? Perhaps this qualifies an individual for the status of true friendship even if he does not live the principles of Stoic wisdom. Epictetus puts it like this:

> You may say, "How can someone have treated me
> well for so long and not love me?" How do you
> know, slave, that he hasn't viewed you in the same
> way he regards the sponge he uses to wipe his
> shoes, or to wash his horse? How do you know
> that, when you have ceased to be useful, he won't
> just throw you away like a broken dish? (II.22.31)

There are just two kinds of life philosophy. There are those that exalt the outer, and those that focus on the inner—those built around taking pleasure in things, and those constructed on the intrinsic virtue of the inner person. Any outer directed individual cannot help but be a user, Epictetus seems to say, and so ultimately cannot be trusted in the fullest way. Only a properly inner directed soul, who values what alone is of intrinsic worth, is solid, stable, and trustworthy enough to be called a friend.

The goodness of a person resides first and foremost in his most fundamental philosophical stance, in the most basic way his will is bent. Epictetus thinks that we'll never get morality or ethics right unless we have the right basic orientation of will, and surround ourselves with as much support for that orientation as possible.

And the support we marshal to help keep ourselves on the right path need not consist in just the friends and companions we choose. Even in our minds, we should associate with the right people. In a discourse on resisting temptation, Epictetus says:

> It's even enough if you withdraw for a moment to the society of noble and just men, and compare yourself with them, whether you find one who is living or dead. (II.18.21)

He then uses the example of Socrates. Epictetus agrees with Seneca in holding that we all need mental exemplars of goodness. In a difficult time of temptation or tough decision-making, we might profit considerably from calling to mind a great person past or present. What would Socrates do? What would Jesus do? How would my father, or mother, make this call? An image of an admired mentor or acknowledged saint can elicit insight and determination within our souls and help us do what is right, however difficult it might be.

If all this does not work, and we still find ourselves yielding to temptation, doing what we ourselves at some level realize to be wrong, Epictetus has a further piece of advice. He says:

> First of all, condemn what you are doing and then, when you have done that, do not despair of yourself. Don't fall into the trap of those men with an inferior spirit who, when they have once given in, then surrender themselves completely and are carried away as if by a torrent. Consider what the trainers of boys do. Has a boy fallen? "Rise," they say, "and wrestle again until you become strong." You should also do something like this. For you can be confident that nothing is more trainable than the human soul. (IV.9.14–16)

No one is perfect. But everyone is, at least in principle, correctible. We are all in a state of becoming. On another occasion, when speaking of our halting attempts to take up the right perspectives on life and to persist in them, Epictetus says:

> Show me a man who is sick and happy, in danger and happy, dying and happy, in exile and happy, in

> disgrace and happy. Show me—I desire, by the gods,
> to see a real Stoic. You can't find one? Then show
> me someone who is becoming like this, who has
> displayed at least a tendency to be a Stoic. (II.19.24–25)

This former slave and determined philosophical liberator is not in the least interested in condemning us for our slip-ups. He is intent on encouraging progress. He does not expect us to be perfectly consistent. He just demands that we try.

We are acquisitive beings. We tend to want it all, and we generally would prefer to have it all now. Whether our desires are directed toward things in the external world, or to inner states of wisdom and virtue, we most often feel like we have to get what we want as quickly as possible. When we are materialists, we are greedy for things. When we become spiritual, we can be fanatical about inner perfection. Epictetus gives us a memorable image:

> To children who put their hand into a narrow
> necked earthen vessel to bring out figs and nuts,
> this often happens: if they fill their hand completely,
> they cannot take it out, and then they cry. Drop a
> little bit and you can draw things out. Do the same
> with your desires. Don't desire too many things and
> you can have what you want. (III.9.22)

Greed is counterproductive. Basic principles of contentment can apply to the realm of the spiritual and ethical as much as they do to the physical domain. It's fine to aspire. It's great to aim high. But we always should be content with making the best progress we can, not despairing of our state, but in all things pressing on toward the most fundamental goal we can set for ourselves, the goal of philosophical freedom and a virtuous will. Epictetus counsels:

> Fortify yourself with contentment, for it is an
> impregnable fortress. (F.CXXXVIII)

Contentment is not acquiescence. It isn't complaisance. It is just the Stoic acceptance that breaks through negative, self-defeating emotions and frees us to act in a way that can make a difference.

The man or woman who has a proper view of externals and of the will, who is at one level content and yet still aspiring, who is surrounded with friends and intent on doing good, is in a position to move into a dimension of human fulfillment too rare in our world: true human excellence. Epictetus reasons:

> What makes a dog beautiful? Possessing the excellence of a dog. And what makes a horse beautiful? Having the excellence of a horse. What then makes a man beautiful? Isn't it having the excellence of a man? And so, if you want to be beautiful, young man, you should work at this: the acquisition of human excellence. But what is that? Pay close attention to the people you praise, when you praise without partiality. Do you praise the just or the unjust? The just. Do you praise the moderate or the excessive? The moderate. Do you praise the self-controlled, or those who are out of control? The self-controlled. If then you make yourself such a person, you can know that you will make yourself beautiful. But as long as you neglect these things, you will really be ugly, no matter how much trouble you take to appear beautiful. (III.1.6–9)

No amount of time in the gym or at the tailor's shop will do the job that inner excellence alone can accomplish. The inner must precede the outer for true human beauty to shine through.

Of course, it may be that Epictetus could never have anticipated how as a world society we would eventually come to value all the wrong things. We live in a time when people do seem all too prone to praise the intemperate and the immoderate. We have a culture that does appear to celebrate the exterior more than the interior of any person. But even now, the more mature an individual is, the more he or she still moves in the direction of approval and disapproval Epictetus is assuming. Our philosopher explains:

> You are not flesh and hair, but you are will. If you make your will beautiful, then you will be beautiful. (223)

Goodness and beauty coincide at the deepest levels of human life.

Epictetus is always most concerned about our general, basic
philosophical orientation to life, but he also gives us many specific
pieces of ethical advice. For example he says such things as:

> What we should not do, we should not even think
> of doing. (F.C)

And

> Think carefully before saying or doing anything,
> for you will not have the power of calling back
> what has been said or done. (F.CI)

Yet, in the final analysis, it is not so much Epictetus's advice on particulars as it is his stance on the general orientation of a human life
that has inspired readers for all these centuries. His assumption is
simple. Once the right overall stance toward life is established, all
the proper particulars will follow.

Epictetus has a view of the good life that allows for a reasonable concept of a good death. The philosopher thinks of us all as
being like guests at a banquet. We should enjoy the repast as long
as it continues, and then thank our host when it ends. He understands that it is natural to fear life's end, but reasons with us about
this in many ways. For instance:

> When death appears to be an evil, we ought to have
> this rule in readiness: that it is right to avoid evil
> things, but death is an unavoidable thing. (1.27.7)

All evils should be avoided. But we cannot avoid death, he reasons,
and so it must not be an evil. Thus, it should be accepted. He himself gives voice to this attitude when he says in another place:

> I must die. If the time is now, then I'm ready. If
> not now, but after a short time, I'll have something
> to eat because it's the lunch hour. After that, I'll die.
> How? Like a man who gives up what belongs to
> another. (1.2.32)

This is ultimate equanimity. Zero anxiety. Nobility of spirit.
Absolute inner resilience.

Epictetus imagines one of his students objecting to all the rigors of Stoic practice, with its relentless concentration on the inner, and apparent looseness of concern with the outer. The young man is especially appalled at the accepting attitude toward mortality. This student is bothered by the mental exercises and perspectives required of him by his Stoic teacher, and in exasperation finally says "Suppose then that I lose my life in this way?" As if philosophy itself could kill. The master teacher replies:

> You will die a good man, doing a noble act. Since
> we must certainly die, of necessity a man must
> be found at that time doing something, either
> following the employment of a farmer, or digging,
> or trading, or serving in a consulship or suffering
> from indigestion or diarrhea. What then do you
> want to be doing when you are caught by death?
> I for my part want to be found doing something
> worthy of a man, something good, suitable to the
> general interest, and noble. (IV.10.11–12)

What more could any of us want? A good death can only come from a good life.

16

NOBLE EXTREMES

Epictetus lays out a full and vivid picture of inner human excellence. He also recommends mental exercises and other practices to cultivate and reinforce that stance in our lives. At one point, he suggests:

> First tell yourself what you want to be, then act consistently with that in everything you do. In nearly all activities we see this at work. Those who follow athletic exercises first determine what they want to be, then they act accordingly. If a man is a long distance runner, there is a certain kind of diet, walking, massage, and exercise. If someone is a sprinter, all these things are different. If he is entering the pentathlon, they are even more different. You'll find the same thing true in the arts. If you are a carpenter, you will have certain things to do, but if you work in metal, other things. If we do anything without a goal in view, we do it to no purpose, and if we do it in connection with the wrong goal, we miss the mark. Furthermore, everyone has a general purpose, and a particular purpose. First, we must act as an authentic human being. (III.23.1–4)

Acting as an authentic human being involves guarding our beliefs, managing our desires, and crafting our emotions, attitudes, and actions around an exalted inner orientation of the soul. We are to focus on the divine spark within us, the faculty of choosing that we call the will, and govern ourselves in such a way that we concentrate on those inner realities that alone we have control over—the actions of the will, as well as its growth in virtue—and adopt an untroubled acceptance, or even a measure of undisturbed indifference, about those externals in life over which we have no control.

Epictetus believes that we were created to be happy, and that happiness requires freedom from anxiety. Anxiety in turn is tied up with any positive valuing of externals, since we can fail to attain them, and be frustrated; we can lose them, and be bereaved; and even when we achieve and continue to have them, we can fear the possibility of losing them, and be anxious. The only true freedom of spirit, he believes, requires a giving up, a yielding, a diverting of attention at some level of desire, yearning, and attachment, so that we loosen our attitudinal and emotional grip on everything in the external world. This is made motivationally possible by a practice of stark and honest reflection on our mortality and on the associated necessities of loss this intrinsically involves, along with an appeal to believe in, and trust, a benevolent God for the course of events that come our way. Epictetus advises each of us:

> Think of God more frequently than you breathe. (F.CXIX)

In a sea of apparent trouble, this loftiness of attention can be our lifeline, and the foundation for our most noble attitudes.

The mindset of inner equanimity and virtue that Epictetus urges on us is surely a noble one. But does he take it to excess? He seems to think it is so important to be liberated from negative emotions that we must avoid totally any positive commitment that might allow them to enter into our lives, should the inevitable happen and something be taken away from us. Let's examine some sample passages that seem to cross a line most of us will not easily join him in crossing. For example, in discussing standard situations of loss, grief, and anger, he tells us:

> Don't admire your clothes and you won't be angry with the thief. Don't admire the beauty of your wife, and you won't be angry with the adulterer. (I.18.11)

It may be of great importance to avoid being victimized by irrational outbursts of anger in our hearts, or seething resentments in our souls, but does it follow from this that it is never appropriate to feel any form of righteous indignation? Can't we develop a form of life where we enjoy our clothes immensely, and yet do not need them with any strong form of attachment that would throw us into an emotional tailspin were they to be taken away? And any recommendation that I not admire my wife's beauty just to see to it that I could never possibly be hurt by her, or by anyone else in their behavior toward her, seems both extreme and wrongheaded.

Epictetus is so concerned with inner growth and inner beauty that he actually says the following about the natural human concern to groom and adorn our physical side:

> What about the body? Leave it as it is by nature. Another has looked after these things: entrust them to him. (III.1.43)

But this, of course, for most of us would not always be a pretty sight. Is a neglect of the body in any way necessary for a nobility of the soul? This certainly seems extreme, and wrong again.

Expressing the general Stoic stance, Epictetus says in one place:

> I have learned to see that everything that happens, if it is independent of my will, is nothing to me. (I.29.24)

But must everything that is not totally within the power of my will be literally "nothing" to me? This is as extreme as we can imagine. Isn't there a category available that would allow things in the world to mean something to us without thereby enslaving us?

Let's see what Epictetus says about our relationship to things, and then how he extends it to cover our relationships to other people. He recommends that

> Whenever you are delighted with anything, don't let your delight be the sort of emotion that would be appropriate only for something that could never be taken away, but make sure it's the kind of emotion appropriate for the sort of thing an earthen pot is, or a glass cup, that, when broken, you can remember what it was and not be troubled. In the same way, when you kiss your own child, or your

> brother or friend, you should never give full license
> to the appearance and allow your pleasure to go as
> far as it chooses, but check it, and curb it, as those
> who stand behind men in their triumphs and
> remind them that they are mortal. You should
> remind yourself in a similar way that the person
> you love is mortal, and that what you love does
> not belong to you. It has been given to you for the
> present, not that it should never be taken away from
> you, and it has not been given to you for all time,
> but rather as a fig is given to you, or a bunch of
> grapes, at the appointed season of the year. If you
> wish for these things in winter, you are a fool. So
> if you wish for your son or friend when it is not
> allowed to you, you must realize that you are
> wishing for a fig in winter. (III.24.84–87)

It is admittedly important for us to monitor how much and in what ways we love things. I believe we can enjoy and even admire physical objects without becoming unduly attached to them. And I say this as a person who has become unreasonably attached to many different things at various times in my life, and who has lived through these experiences in such a way as to come to see my excesses and change my attitude.

Shortly after I had bought my first convertible, a sparkling, beautiful BMW that had become my pride and joy, it was adorned, one day while parked, with a series of eighteen significant dents along one side. When I saw the damage, I was sick at heart. I found myself experiencing a measure of shock, sadness and even depression that I later came to view as completely absurd and totally incommensurate with the proper status of any such physical object in a person's life. My reaction was perhaps a common one—which just shows how pervasive this problem is—but I realized right away that I had to come to my senses and change my fundamental attitude to physical things in the world. Not that I had to cease enjoying physical beauty, or stop taking care of the things that I owned, but I had to learn how to relate to beautiful physical objects in a manner more appropriate to their true status in life. I needed to free myself from a dependency I had not even been aware I was suffering from until that event, which stopped me in my tracks and brought with it my needed self-revelation.

The North Carolina mountain man, Eustace Conway, immortalized in Elizabeth Gilbert's book, *The Last American Man*, tells a story about hiking alone in Glacier National Park, above the timberline, walking across a snow belt. Uncharacteristically, he lost his footing and fell, sliding fast down a steep slope on his back, unable to stop. Without an ice ax or any real gear, he tried every trick he knew to slow his fall, pressing his backpack into the ice as he slid, attempting to dig in his heels to break his speed, but nothing worked. He was hurtling backwards over snow and gravel and rocks, completely out of control, realizing that death was a possible outcome of all this, when suddenly he slammed into something that instantly brought him to a total, jarring stop. He got up and was amazed to see that he had slid into the side of a dead mule—a large, frozen, mummified mule. As he looked up from the mule, he saw they were both just feet away from a cliff and a two thousand foot drop he had been heading straight for, out of control, and unable to see. If he hadn't hit the dead mule, he would have plunged to his death in such a remote location that, he says, no one would have found his body for a thousand years.

After fifteen years of teaching at Notre Dame, I left to set up my own shop as a philosopher. I had no idea that my annual income would actually increase by many multiples as I found new ways to bring people the great ideas of the ages. Philosophers do what we do because we are impelled to, not because it pays the bills. For most philosophers, it doesn't. I had become a philosopher first because that's just who I am, and second, because I wanted to accomplish a distinctive form of good in people's lives. But now, in addition to being able to do good on a broad scale, I was suddenly and unexpectedly able to enjoy things that, as a professor, I would not even have considered wanting. For the first time, I could buy, use, and immensely enjoy well made cars, fine mechanical watches, beautiful fountain pens, comfortable suits, great shoes, and countless other goodies I had never even dreamed of owning. I realized very soon that I love and appreciate the aesthetics of excellent craftsmanship. I really loved all this stuff. But I loved it too much. I wasn't aware that I was sliding fast down a steep mountain in the direction of a sheer spiritual cliff.

Those eighteen dents in my new car were my dead mule. They stopped me in my tracks. I got up, looked around, realized where I had been heading, and changed my inner direction dramatically. I didn't come to think there is anything inherently wrong with nice things, or with owning and enjoying them, but I came to realize that enjoyable physical objects can easily enslave us unless we are careful to cultivate the right fundamental attitude toward them.

Epictetus is right to think we should not grasp on to physical things with a dependency attachment that entangles our souls. Any failure to recognize this is a great danger to the soul. But does it follow from this that we should not care deeply about the health or life of people with whom we are in close relationships? Aren't people very different from things? Let's look at one more passage on this. Epictetus says:

> We can learn the will of nature from the things in which we do not differ from one another. For example, when your neighbor's slave has broken his cup, or anything else, we are ready to say right then that this is just one of those things that happen. You should know then that when your cup is broken you should think as you did when your neighbor's was broken. Then transfer this reaction to greater things. Is another man's child or wife dead? There is no one who would not say that this is something that happens to people. But when a man's own wife or child is dead, right then he says, "Woe to me, how wretched I am!" But we should remember exactly how we feel when we hear that it has happened to others. (E.XXVI)

Here our philosopher offers us a technique to rid ourselves of emotionally negative reactions to such events as the death of a spouse or a child. Are we really to greet such an event with undisturbed equanimity? Is no grief appropriate at all? In many passages, Epictetus implies this. Here he offers another technique:

> When you're kissing your child or your wife, tell yourself that this is a human being you are kissing, for then when the wife or child dies, you will not be disturbed. (E.III)

Our philosopher goes even farther in one passage of self reflection and says:

> There is no intimate relationship between my father
> and me, but there is between the good and me.
> (III.3.5)

In saying such things, Epictetus may surely be going to extremes
into which we need not follow him, while yet reaping the benefits
of his otherwise extraordinarily important and sensible advice.

The general principle throughout, as always, is this:

> When you hear any report that could be disturbing,
> have this principle in readiness—the news is not
> about anything within the power of your will.
> (III.18.1)

Anything outside the power of my will is not to disturb me at all.
This frees me from the enslavements of desire and fear, and it
allows for a nobility of inner purity unthreatened by the exigencies
of life. It is such an extremity of view that prompts Epictetus to say:

> Is life a good thing? No. Is death a bad thing? No.
> Is prison? No. (IV.1.133)

Nothing outside the will and its power is intrinsically good or bad
in the eyes of our radical philosopher of freedom.

But what do we really think of this view? What are its implica-
tions? What are its limits? Epictetus is indeed a liberator. He offers
powerful reasons and techniques to free us from emotional ties and
attitudes that do tend to hold us back in life, inhibit our proper arcs
of achievement, and even corrupt our souls. But do we indeed
have to throw out the proverbial baby with the bathwater? To elim-
inate a pain in your finger, do you need to cut off your arm? Can't
we draw some important distinctions here? I think that indeed we
can.

By his own principles, Epictetus will acknowledge that people
are centers of choosing. People are souls. People are wills. If wills
are intrinsically important, then people are intrinsically important.
But Epictetus says that something can be good or evil only if it is
within the power of the will. And the wills of others, along with
their very existence in this world, are certainly not matters wholly
within the power of our wills. Epictetus, however, believes in God,
and urges us all to do so as well. And God is the paradigmatic Will,

the creator and governor of all. We could suggest to Epictetus that, on his own principles, the existence of other human wills on this earth is a matter within the power of God's will and thus falls within the realm of good and evil. The life or death of another person then can indeed be viewed as being, or at least as involving, a good or bad thing. And as any good can properly be rejoiced over and any bad can appropriately be grieved, the lives and deaths of other people can properly evoke within us such emotions and attitudes.

This sort of argument would have to be developed further and qualified in various ways to pass all the tests of the strictest philosophical legitimacy. But my point here is only that it can be done. We can go much of the distance with Epictetus, and then at a certain point logically part company with our guide. The completely legitimate and vital point that our philosopher's ruminations still bring to our attention is that there are limits to the nature of our proper emotional attachments, and bounds to the magnitude and extent of appropriate grief. But they are perhaps much farther out than Epictetus would prefer to allow.

My colleague's son dies in a terrible accident. The father and mother grieve. The whole community is shocked and saddened. Anything less would fail to acknowledge the intrinsic importance of their son's life, and of the earthly relationships with him that suddenly are ended with his death. From many religious and philosophical points of view, the boy's death need not, and should not, be viewed as the cessation of his existence, or as the absolute terminus of all personal relationships with him. He will continue to exist, in another form, and on another plane of reality. And the deepest love relationships to him will be able to continue, in faith for the meantime, in the lives of those left behind, and then, one day again, in some sense face to face. The interim of bereavement is properly one of sadness and grief, but tempered by faith and hope.

The tragedy that I allude to is one recounted by the wonderful man and penetrating philosopher, Nicholas Wolterstorff, in his moving book, *Lament for a Son*. As a Christian, Wolterstorff had fundamental worldview beliefs that allowed him a hope for the future. But they did not prevent, and should not have eliminated, his experience of grief in the aftermath of his son's death. The sudden loss of a loved one properly evokes grief and sadness. But the sufferer with an overarching philosophy of life and a set of fundamental commitments that evoke hope and trust in a redeeming providential guidance will grieve within limits. His sadness will not altogether unhinge him for life. He will not be forever enslaved by despondency. He will honor the departed loved one in his heart, and then learn to move forward in life once again.

Epictetus believed that a philosopher is a physician for the soul. But he need not be an overachieving anesthesiologist. Our goal should not be to deaden the emotions completely. We need only take the edge off the pain, so that life can go on while the healing begins. All the psychological techniques Epictetus gives us can be used in service to moderation and need not be geared toward a total extirpation of the passionate side of life. By saying this, I am suggesting a more Aristotelian perspective on the emotions that is also more in line with the Judeo-Christian tradition. The Stoics most often go to extremes on the topic of emotional connection. They may in some sense be noble extremes, but they are extremes indeed.

We can understand the transitory nature of life, and allow this understanding to inform our emotions, attitudes, and actions, while trusting ourselves and our fortunes to the benevolent oversight of an ultimately dependable providence, without also assigning the external world, and things in the world, a value of zero. We can learn to transcend the moment, put things in perspective, calm down, and act with honor, without pretending that nothing matters in the end outside the confines of our innermost souls. The path of personal strength doesn't require that we not care about anything in the external world around us, it only requires that we care about the right things in the right ways.

We can thank Epictetus, our philosophical liberator and great physician of the soul, for his profound insights, for his vivid lessons, and for his concern over our inner freedom, without necessarily drawing every conclusion that he himself drew about life. The perspectives he gave us can still act as profound preparations for our individual journeys of achievement in this world. That's generally the way it is when we benefit from the advice of other people. The wisest among us never get it all right. Thus, we are always called upon to separate the wheat from the chaff, the wisdom from the error. We can throw away the packaging, while keeping the great gift we have been given, even if it has to be resized to fit our needs. We then can enjoy that gift for life.

PART III

WISE WORDS ON LIFE STRAIGHT FROM THE TOP

*The Imperial Insights of
Marcus Aurelius*

17

A THINKER IN CHARGE

Marcus Aurelius was born in A.D. 121 and became Emperor of Rome at the age of forty. He had enjoyed the benefits of a good family life, a strong upbringing, and a fine philosophical education, all of which prepared him well for holding the highest public office in perhaps the greatest of empires at a time of tremendous political turmoil and war.

This philosopher is known to history as a successful military leader, despite his peaceful temperament, and as a wise political ruler who oversaw the Golden Age of Rome. He was married and was an avid lifelong student as well as a man of action. At the pinnacle of human power in his time, Emperor Marcus Aurelius Antoninus, as he is officially known to historians, showed a disposition of personal humility and integrity in how he governed, as well as in how he wrote. His only major lapse in judgment as a leader seems to have been his sanction of a measure of religious persecution for the Christian movement, which he never personally had occasion to understand on a philosophical or theological level.

This busy general took time during his military campaigns to sit up late at night and write down his observations about life in a personal notebook. These "Meditations" have become one of the most popular expressions of Stoic philosophy ever published. With them, he became the last great Stoic thinker and writer of antiquity.

I find it interesting that Marcus Aurelius had his insights about life, and wrote them down, while out on military campaigns. He wasn't in his study, or in the comfort of a palace. He was living an adventure, facing danger, making difficult decisions, and dealing with the occasionally unpleasant consequences of those choices. I believe there is in this a lesson for us all. It is in our most difficult times, metaphorically fighting the battles of life, that we often gain the most valuable wisdom of all.

I don't find myself in agreement with absolutely everything this royal sage says, but I do find a great deal of his thought to be as applicable to life here at the beginning of a new millennium as it was during his own day, almost two millennia ago. In his writings, he is concerned with both our inner experience of life and our outer actions. He has much to say to people living in times of dramatic change, and many of his reflections counterbalance quite forcefully some unfortunate tendencies most of us, at some time or other, find in ourselves, tendencies toward allowing negative emotions, such as worry, irritation, frustration, anger and impatience with anything that gets in our way to derail us from our proper attitude and course through life. The emperor's positive advice is particularly powerful on issues relating to personal achievement and lasting success, a subject with which he was, of course, intimately familiar.

As a philosopher living almost two thousand years later, I have come to believe that long lasting, deeply satisfying success in our lives is facilitated by following a few simple but profound universal recommendations, or philosophical guidelines, that can apply to any situation we ever might face. Marcus, in his time, saw that we need guidelines to help us achieve and sustain a good and successful life. He sometimes wrote of life as being like a war, at other times of its being like a sojourn in a strange place. He recognized that, with all the challenges we inevitably face in this world, we need help in finding our way forward. He saw the enterprise or activity of philosophy as giving us the basic principles for living that will accomplish just that. Repeating a kind of comparison that was often used in the ancient world, he says:

> As physicians have always their instruments and knives ready for cases which suddenly require their skill, so do you have principles ready for the understanding of things divine and human, and doing everything, even the smallest, with a recollection of the bond which unites the divine and human to one another. (III.13)

In context, we find that he meant something very simple. We need intellectual and practical tools to help us in everything we do, for nothing is ultimately unimportant. Everything should be viewed within the context of the biggest of big pictures, and that broad perspective should guide us in the use we make of the philosophical tools we have. He specifies:

> What, then, is able to guide a man? There is one thing, and only one—philosophy. (II.17)

In Marcus's view, it is philosophy that gives us our bearings. It reminds us of the ultimate context for all our decisions and all our actions. It provides us with the big picture that we all need.

At one point he offers the advice:

> Think often about the connection between all things in the universe and their relation to each other. (VI.38)

He believes that we need regular reminders of our context. Everything is connected at the most ultimate level. A mindfulness of these connections can guide us along our way. It is forgetfulness of context that is behind so many of our problems. That's why Marcus views philosophy as such a problem solver. It provides perspective. And there is hardly anything as powerful in this life as a proper perspective.

At one point in his notes, Marcus exclaims:

> How small a part of the boundless and unfathomable stretch of time is assigned to every man! In just a moment, it is swallowed up in eternity. And how small a piece of the universal substance! How tiny a part of the universal soul! And on what a small clod of the whole earth you crawl! Reflecting on all this, consider nothing to be great, except to act as your nature leads you, and to endure that which the common nature brings. (XII.32)

Philosophy provides perspective and it guides us back to our own deepest nature as the truly proper wellspring of all that we do. It points us in the direction of what we all most need for the genuine achievement in our lives that we so desire.

18

INNER GUIDANCE

We've already seen what the Stoic thinker Seneca had to say about appropriate and well-directed goal setting. Marcus Aurelius emphasizes that, in order to move forward in this life in all the right ways, we regularly need to give ourselves the great gift of time to think and reassess our priorities. We need the inner guidance that can arise only out of regular and sustained personal reflection.

In recent years, many people have come to realize the importance of looking within to find their deepest resources. Because of this, busy people in many walks of life have taken to going on personal retreats, or spiritual getaways that will make this meditative time possible. As a consequence, in the past few years, some of the monasteries and spiritual retreat centers in America have had lower vacancy rates on weekends than major hotel chains.

But Marcus doesn't think it's necessary to have a spiritual hideaway. Correcting his own tendencies to feel otherwise, he writes a note to himself that:

> Men are always looking for retreats in the country, at the beach, and in the mountains. You want it as much as anyone. But this is a common mistake. It's completely within your power, whenever you choose, to retreat into yourself. (IV.3)

Examine your own heart, explore you own innermost thoughts, he advises himself and the rest of us. Get to know yourself right now wherever you are. What are your strengths? What are your weaknesses? What do you want to make happen? What do you need to let go? What are your deepest values? What means the most to you? What principles will steer you on your path? These issues can be confronted at any place, and at almost any time, if you'll give yourself periods of quiet isolation from the telephone, the television, the computer, and the many demands of the day.

Marcus Aurelius continues:

> Give yourself this sort of retreat as often as you need to, and use it to renew your spirit. Reminding yourself of your basic beliefs, principles, and values will be enough to refresh your soul and send you back into the world free from discontent with the things to which you return. (IV.3)

We need to make basic commitments that will guide and constrain all that we do, and we should remind ourselves regularly of what these commitments are. Marcus, like Epictetus, is aware of the importance of freedom in this life. But the deepest freedom is never freedom from having basic value commitments. It is rather our deepest commitments that free us from unnecessary entanglements and activities that do not express who we most truly are.

Getting in touch with our own dreams, desires, aspirations, goals, and values is never to be thought of as a once-and-for-all experience, or even as a rare interlude in our active lives. We need to retreat within ourselves again and again to renew and refresh our sense of where we are heading and how we will get there. The measure of self-knowledge we need for guidance in decision-making must be a growing thing, renewed on a regular, or frequent, basis.

In another passage, Marcus admonishes himself to "return to philosophy frequently and repose in her, through whom what you meet with in the court will appear to you tolerable, and you will appear tolerable in the court." Philosophy makes the man—and, of course, the woman. It can present life in a more palatable form to us, helping us to deal with anything we confront, and it in turn can empower us to present ourselves in a better way to life.

Marcus would have us take care about what we choose first and foremost to pursue in this world. A little philosophy on the proper ends of life will suffice to produce some simple and penetrating realizations. Money alone will never satisfy—nor will power, fame or status. The only wealth certain to fulfill us is inner wealth, a sort of health of the spirit, manifested in proper attitudes, emotions, and thoughts. And it is inner wealth that most easily flows over into the outer world in sustainable accomplishment.

If Marcus were asked, I think he would say that our personal goal setting in this world must always take account of the inner person. What are we chasing, and why? Where will it take us as people? What will we become in virtue of pursuing and attaining the goals that we set? How can we build great and sustainable good in everything we do?

Our Emperor understands the lure of external things. All the Stoics were insistent that we distinguish between those externals that never fully satisfy and the inner wealth that alone gives happiness and meaning. Marcus, in his position, especially understands the lure of fame, celebrity, or renown. Many people value money as much because of the esteem it buys as for any of its other functions. The same is true of power, and also of social status. A craving for approval, for human acceptance and praise, can come to have an inordinate importance and motivating power in all that we do. The philosopher counsels:

> It could be that a desire for fame pulls at you. But think for a minute about how soon everything is forgotten. Consider the abyss of infinite time on each side of the present moment. Remember the typical hollowness of applause, and the fickleness of most of the people who offer anyone else praise. And finally call to mind the tiny stage on which this all takes place. The whole earth is just a point, and your particular place on it is much smaller still. Be realistic about the number of people who ever will praise you, and what they're really like. (IV.3)

And, later,

> What then is genuinely worth being valued? To be received with a clapping of hands? No, and we shouldn't value a flapping of tongues either. Let's face it—any praise that comes from the multitude is just a flapping of tongues. Now, if you give up the worthless thing called fame, you'll see that what remains can truly be worth valuing. All that really matters is to move yourself and restrain yourself in conformity with your own nature—and this is the proper purpose of all the arts and occupations. (VI.16)

Here's the way I like to put it. It's a 3D approach to life achievement:

(1) Discover your talents.

(2) Develop those talents.

(3) Deploy your talents into the world for the good of others as well as yourself.

Don't aim primarily at external, extrinsic rewards, even though you are often pursuing external goals. Don't make your primary concern wealth, fame, power, or status. If you concentrate instead on becoming what you are most deeply capable of being, and on doing good by making your own distinctive contribution to the other people in this world, you'll ironically be much more likely to get any of those external things that you really need for the next step in your journey.

Here is a point Marcus sometimes overlooks. He's so busy deflecting our attention away from the externals we so naturally obsess over that he neglects to point out how externals can often very appropriately enter the mix. Sometimes the applause and praise of others is one of your best indications that you're serving them well. Sometimes. And, on occasion, that very support will help you to take your enterprise to the next level. Others will want to be a part of what you're doing. They will be eager to help. Acceptance, praise, and even fame can facilitate and empower, but only as long as they do not ever lure us away from what is right for our inner constitution, only as long as they don't distract us away from our distinctive inner nature, or cause us in any way to betray who we most deeply are.

The same is true of financial reward. It can be both a sign that we are doing good, and a resource for doing more. Marcus is so concerned about our tendency to fixate on the external to the exclusion of the internal, that he inclines to err in the opposite direction, like a man walking on a high wall, who overcorrects for a sense that he will fall in one direction by leaning too far to the opposite side, and then falling indeed. But real balance in wisdom requires that we recognize all facets of the truth.

The path to personal power involves setting goals that are right for you. Engage in enterprises that are well matched to your personal constitution. Pursue ends that resonate with your innermost nature. Steer your way by principles that matter. And create your own unique form of good for the world—in your home, your neighborhood, your town, and your business. That way, you can serve your fellow human beings in the best possible manner, and grow to make your proper addition to the universe.

DEALING WITH DIFFICULTY AND CHANGE

Marcus Aurelius is not about to be held back, or daunted, by difficulty. He advises:

> **If something is difficult, don't conclude too
> quickly that it's impossible. It's better to assume
> that whatever is possible at all is within your
> personal reach as well.** (IV.19)

Marcus encourages us to think big. His advice is meant to empower. It's truly incredible how many people hold themselves back in life because of groundless beliefs that their dreams are impossible, or that they couldn't conceivably do something that is in itself well within the reach of human accomplishment. We limit ourselves in ways that are unnecessary. The Emperor believes in a can-do approach to life.

Anyone who takes the philosopher's recommendation to think big will soon need a second piece of his advice. Don't let the naysayers get you down. Every dream has its detractors. Don't be quick to yield to the negative opinions of other people who might express significant doubts about your prospects in life, or in a particular project. Too often, we allow ourselves to be bullied by the opinions of others. To be true to ourselves, we must learn to resist this tendency and cultivate an inner resilience of confidence that can stand firm, whatever others may say.

Marcus reflects:

> **I have often found it strange that every man loves
> himself more than anyone else, and yet values his**

own opinion of himself less than the opinions others have about him. (XII.4)

We need to habituate ourselves to thoughts that empower, not
to thoughts that unduly limit. Marcus remarks that:

> Whatever your habitual thoughts are like will
> determine the character of your mind. Your soul
> will take on the particular color of your thoughts.
> (V.16)

Your life is what your thoughts make it. That is why it is important
for all of us to guard our minds from unhealthy habits of thinking,
habits that hold us back from what we could be accomplishing.
And what is so insidious about bad habits of thought is that we are
so accustomed to thinking with them that we often find it difficult
to think about them. We are often not aware that we even have
unproductive habits of thought until they are brought to our attention by someone else.

One of the most common causes for the mental habits of anxiety, worry, hesitancy, or simple lack of confidence these days is the
pace of change people feel themselves to be experiencing in an
ongoing, seemingly relentless way. We often fear change, or at least
find our self-confidence undermined by it. Marcus asks:

> Are you ever afraid of change? But what can
> take place without it? What in the whole universe
> is more natural than change? Can you even take
> a bath unless the wood that heats the water
> undergoes a change? Can you be nourished by
> food unless it goes through a change? And
> can anything else useful be accomplished without
> change? You should realize that change is as
> necessary for you as it is for the rest of the
> universe. (VII.18)

Often Marcus directs our thoughts to the natural world, what nature
does, the needs of human nature, and what our most basic individual nature requires. He believes that most of our problems arise
when we depart from the requirements of nature. He counsels:

> Remember that philosophy requires only what your
> own nature needs. But you often desire something
> that's not required by nature. (V.9)

Philosophy, according to the Stoics, directs us to examine our own basic nature and to act in accordance with it. It never demands that we act contrary to nature. Our errors and illusions flout who we most fundamentally are. Philosophy calls us back from them by calling us back to the simple truth.

Many people meet with change the way a bug meets a fast moving windshield. It's not a pretty result. But Marcus wants to give us the big picture for change:

> Look around you and you'll notice that all things
> take place by change. Get used to the idea that the
> nature of the universe loves nothing as much as to
> change the things that are and to make new things
> like them. (IV.36)

From this he concludes that:

> It is not bad for things to change, and not
> necessarily good for things to remain as they are
> after a change. (IV.42)

Once we are fully aware of the cosmic shell game of creativity, impermanence, and further novelty that the universe is playing, even so near to us as to be within us, we can take up a new and more positive view of this universal flow. Seek therefore not permanence, but prepare to meet change by initiating further change—creating, growing, and flourishing as a result. There really is no other game in town.

But if change is so fundamental, if it is one of the few constants in the deep fabric of life, and we inform our attitudes vividly with this fact, we can resist that great common temptation to react negatively to its prospect, and instead grasp its reality boldly, confidently moving forward with the talents and experiences we have. Our talents and experiences are the natural equipment we have been given precisely for the purpose of embracing change and using it well.

If we are engaging in proper goal setting, initiating changes ourselves, and dealing confidently with whatever unexpected changes come our way, we can daily move in the direction of making our most appropriate mark on the world. Our philosophical guide would not want us to settle for anything less.

20

MAKING OUR WAY
FORWARD

As we set goals rooted in self-knowledge, and confidently move in the direction of the forms of achievement that we have envisioned for ourselves, we naturally make plans for the process that we see as most likely to get us to those goals. But we live in a world of unexpected challenge and change. The Stoics recognized that a crucial element in any rational planning process is ongoing adaptability, the capacity to flex and adjust as new obstacles or opportunities come our way.

Speaking of the inner mind of the successful person, Marcus Aurelius contends:

> The inner spirit that directs our lives, when it's
> functioning in accordance with nature, can adapt
> well to whatever happens, and can respond easily
> to what is possible and what is available. It doesn't
> need any one specific material for its use, but it
> can pursue its purposes as any of the external
> circumstances confronting it may allow. It can
> turn even difficult obstacles into opportunities, just
> as a fire can respond to wood that is thrown on
> to it. The amount of wood that could smother and
> extinguish a very small flame can be used by a strong
> enough fire and can make it rise even higher. (IV.1)

This is a great image. Our obstacles can become fuel for our enterprise, if the fire that burns within us is big enough—if we are committed enough and therefore strong enough. We can benefit from even our mistakes and the difficult surprises that sometimes suddenly come to stand in our way if we are attuned to learning from them and taking any new raw materials they throw in our direction as potential fuel for the next stage of the process.

Wise people are opportunistic in the best possible sense. They are always looking for positive opportunities, for openings in the world, for unexpected paths that might advantageously be used in support of the noble goals they are pursuing. The counsel of wisdom here is simple. In a world of challenge and constant yet unpredictable change, we need a flexible and adaptive mindset that will allow us to move forward in the most effective ways.

We also need a mindset that takes account of little things. Marcus admonishes:

> It is your job to order your life well in every single action, and then to be content with how each of those actions does its job. No one can keep any of your actions from playing its proper role in your life. —"But something external may stand in my way."—Nothing will stand in the way of your acting with justice, self-control, and good sense. —"But some obstacle might keep me from getting the results I want."—By accepting the situation as it is and being content to transfer your efforts to what is possible, another opportunity for action will appear in the place of what was hindered, and it will be one that will adapt itself to this ordering of which we are speaking. (VIII.32)

Notice the point here. Marcus reminds us that all we are responsible for in our quest for achievement is doing our very best in the effort we make. We can't guarantee that any particular strategy or process we have launched will attain the results we hope for. Something may get in the way. But if we do not let that cause us frustration, a negative emotional state which just makes alternate planning that much more difficult, if we remain as calm and as content as possible, accepting what has happened and determining to learn and benefit from it, we make it much more likely that we will be able to see new pathways of action that subsequently open up to us, previously unanticipated directions of activity toward the goal where our best efforts can indeed prevail.

Eastern philosophers have always liked the image of water in this regard. When moving water encounters an obstacle, it just runs around it, using the spaces that are available. It is flexible and adaptive, as we all should be.

The Stoics consistently urge us to view whatever happens as somehow being within the will of God, whether we like it or not. At times, their reassurances based on divine providence can even sound a bit fatalistic, as if the ultimate sequencing of events in this world is totally outside our control. But this passage from Marcus gives us another perspective. We should accept whatever happens, even if it appears to block our way forward, not just because of some cosmic unimportance to any potentially frustrating event, and not just by a generic reliance on a rational providence, but because it positively challenges our creativity to learn, adapt, and perform in otherwise unanticipated and novel ways.

One of the most common emotions in our world is frustration. Especially among those of us concerned to make a positive difference in this life, frustration, irritation, and annoyance in response to perceived obstacles ironically become the biggest obstacles to an effective use of our energy. It is no surprise then that the most perspicacious of the Stoic philosophers were very concerned to help us deal with and overcome our tendency toward these negative inner states.

One overall negative emotional state the Stoics were very concerned about, as we have seen, is anger. Here, again, where most of us are tempted to fret and fume over anything we don't like that happens to cross our paths, the Stoic predilection is for pragmatic action, where action is possible, and inner acceptance where it is not. Consider this somewhat surprising passage from the Emperor, certainly a quotation to show to anyone who thinks that philosophers do not address practical issues:

> Are you angry with a man whose armpits stink?
> Are you angry with one who has really bad breath?
> What good will this anger do you? With a mouth
> like that, and with those armpits, it is necessary that
> such emanations arise.—"But the man has a mind
> too," you might reply, "and he is certainly capable
> of realizing how offensive he is."—I wish you well
> with your discovery. You have a mind, too, and can
> reason. Use your mind to awaken his. Point out to
> him what he's doing wrong. Be his teacher. If he

listens, you will solve the problem, and there will be
no need of anger. (V.28)

We can safely fill in some suppressed reasoning here. In context,
the argument seems to be this. If someone offends you, your reaction of disapproval is either rational or it's irrational. If it's irrational,
then you should realize that, change your reaction and drop any
anger you might feel. If it's rational, then you have an option other
than feeling anger, and a better one. The person offending you is
himself either rational or he is irrational. If he is irrational, then he
bothers you only in the way a strong wind, a heavy rain, or a sting-
ing mosquito would, and is therefore not a proper object of hostility. But if he is rational, all you need to do is diplomatically point
out the cause of offense, and he will respond appropriately, remov-
ing the cause of difficulty by his change, in which case again there
is again no room for anger. Anger is thus either unnecessary or
superfluous, and should here, as always, be replaced by acceptance or action.

The Emperor's reasoning is fascinating. He seems to be saying
that an awkward conversation always beats stewing over something you don't like, as long as you are in the company of rational people. But in such company, why should the conversation be
awkward in the first place? Admonish wrong doers well and help
them get on the right path. Don't wallow in negative emotions or
attitudes.

In common parlance, to have a Stoic reaction to a situation—
especially to a provocation or difficulty—is to rise above it, to transcend the moment in such a way as not to feel any negative emotions as a result of it. We often think of the Stoics as steeling themselves against such things as frustration, irritation, annoyance,
anger, despair, grief, and sadness by inner thought techniques productive of perspective and a dismissive attitude. They weren't,
however, working primarily to prevent bad emotions from having
bad effects. They were seeking to avoid, and to help us avoid, having such emotions in the first place. And they encouraged the asking of simple but penetrating questions for this purpose.

Whenever we encounter difficulties, we are encouraged by the
Stoics to ask such questions as: "What is this, in the context of eter-
nity?" and "Who is going to care about this in a thousand years?"
Whenever the drama of our lives takes an unexpected and unwel-
come turn, we are urged to think such things as: "This whole mess

is taking place on a minuscule stage on the infinitesimally small clod of earth that we know as our temporary home, within the overarching context of an unimaginably huge, yawning cosmos. What difference does this little unpredicted side show ultimately make?"

Related to this is the thought: "So things seem bad today? Wait a short time and they'll change." Marcus recommends:

> Think about the speed with which things come and go, pass by and disappear—both the things that are around now and those that are yet to be. The world is like a river in continual flow, the activities of things are in constant change, and causes work in infinite varieties. There is hardly anything that stands still. And consider something else very near to you, the boundless abyss of the past and the endless stretch of the future in which all things vanish. Only a real fool is puffed up by things, or worried about them, or miserable because of them. Any problem that arises lasts only for a time, and really for just a very short time. (V.23)

Perspective can work wonders. Many frazzled leaders have hung on to the simple motto, "This too shall pass." The wheel turns. And if we are patient, we find new ways to attain our goals and make our proper contributions to the world. But a Stoic thinker would always issue a cautionary note. Perhaps we are here primarily for the inner creativity of great effort itself, and not to guarantee any particular set of external results. We are here to attain the inner excellence that eventually will find a way to reflect itself into the outer world, however that reflection is cast. Inner resilience cannot guarantee any particular set of outer results, but it can put us into the best possible position for the greatest results that are within our reach.

21

CONQUERING LIFE'S DISTRACTIONS

How should we deal with the distractions of life that threaten to derail our progress? How can we attain real consistency in living our values and pursuing our goals? What will allow us to maintain our proper path throughout times of difficulty and circumstances of significant temptation? Is there a best way of developing the inner strength and harmony that will best position us for success?

Many of the Stoic thinkers recognized the value of consistency in our behavior as we move forward in life. We need to govern our decisions and actions, as well as our emotions and attitudes, so that they stay consonant with our deepest beliefs and values, as well as with the proper goals, aspirations, and dreams toward which we are moving. And yet there is hardly anything more common in human life than inconsistent behavior. We act out of step with our own values. We do something that is deeply self-defeating, or even self-destructive. We waste our time. We squander our energies. Why? How could inconsistency ever creep into a life? There are many openings and so many answers to this question.

Distraction, laziness, pressure, temptation, rationalization, and vagueness are just a few of the causes of action inconsistent with our settled goals. Marcus focuses in on a couple of these. Sometimes inconsistency arises from a sort of thoughtlessness, acting without sufficiently considering what exactly we are doing and why we are doing it. We can surprise ourselves with the inconsistency of our own behavior at times when sheer thoughtlessness has held sway in our choices.

Occasionally, we can let narrowly selfish motives interfere with our properly higher goals. Marcus addresses both these problems, of thoughtlessness and selfishness, when he counsels:

> First, do nothing without thinking it through and
> having a purpose. Second, make sure your actions
> always serve a social end. (XII.20)

Appropriately social ends are goals that take seriously the interests of other people, and are, the philosopher believes, sustainable with consistency. Selfish ends, he seems to think, are not. A blending of the two is certainly an unstable mix.

It's important for us to make a simple distinction here. Selfishness is not the same thing as self-interestedness, or self-concern. A healthy concern over, and attention to, your own good need not ever be out of step with broader social goals and values. And it need not ever generate internal inconsistency in your actions. Selfishness is by definition an unhealthy exclusiveness of self-interest that ignores the real needs and legitimate interests of other people, and that also, ironically, leads to self-destructive behavior. The well-known and profound moral advice to "Love your neighbor as yourself" presupposes a perfectly natural and acceptable self-regard as its foundation. But when we pursue literally selfish goals, we move into a territory where behavior inconsistent with any higher ideals, broader aims, and our own true good is guaranteed.

Marcus urges us to see to it that all our actions are purposive, and that they all support both high ideals and broad social needs. We ourselves are happier living and working among other people who are happy. We experience our greatest personal good in a context where we respect and support the appropriate goods that other people need and pursue. Behavior inconsistent with the broader needs of our communities, and with our own deepest personal needs, can certainly creep into our lives. But when we spot it, we need to do something about it.

What then can get us on the track of consistent living and keep us there? Speaking in another passage about the person who has learned well from a study of philosophy, our royal advisor claims that he is

> He is content with these two things: acting justly
> in what he does, and being satisfied with what he
> faces. He lays aside all distracting and busy pursuits,
> and desires nothing more than to achieve the

straight path through the law, and by accomplishing
the straight course, to follow God. (X.11)

Laying aside all distracting and busy pursuits. How difficult and
how crucial this is. Time management has always been an issue for
busy people, in the ancient world as well as in the present. And it's
probably no exaggeration to say that time mis-management is one
of the most pervasive sources of inconsistent behavior in our day.
We act inconsistently when we do not do what we should do when
we should do it, allowing "distracting and busy pursuits" to derail
us from the straight path we should be taking to our goals. How
do we resist the tyranny of the trivial urgent? How do we withstand
the pull of fear, the inertia of laziness, and the lure of easy pleas-
ures that tempt us into inconsistency? Our wise advisor has an
answer.

A satisfied mind and a just practice are here laid out as the two
most important elements in our effort "to follow God" by "accomplishing the straight course," in other words, to bring about the best
of what we are in this world to achieve by consistently pursuing
our highest vision and goals. Don't be derailed by troubles. And
don't be sidetracked by temptations. How? Build inner peace and
hold on to justice as the foundation for outer results of great good.
That is the Stoic's advice.

It's common for many of us to be buffeted about by negative
emotions as we encounter difficulties, and to be tempted in
response to these emotions to act out of character, blowing up,
seeking revenge, taking the low road, cutting corners, losing our
focus, or just giving up. Marcus Aurelius has a simple strategy for
dealing with times such as these. Look at the Big Picture. Take a
deep breath (my elaboration), and put the situation into perspective. Transcend the moment and contextualize it in the broadest
possible way.

It's a general human tendency to react badly to perceived hurts.
When someone does something to harm or insult us, we get mad.
And the anger grows. Pretty soon, we're doing and saying things
that we otherwise would never do and say. The anger has taken
over. We have become its puppet. We are no longer in control of
ourselves. And this means that, whatever the original harm might
have been, we have made it worse by our reaction. It's as if in
response to being shot with an arrow, we pull it out, put a bit of

poison on its tip, and stick it back into the wound, making things worse. But to put it in these terms is to see right away how irrational the whole reaction is.

Marcus Aurelius does not want this to happen. If anyone does something with an apparently negative impact on you, Marcus would have you consider several distinct possibilities that may not otherwise immediately come to mind, any one of which can change the way you feel about the wrong:

(1) Maybe he didn't intend to do it at all,

or

(2) Perhaps he acted in ignorance of the consequences for you,

or

(3) The situation might not be as bad as it at first seems,

or

(4) It may end up as a gain rather than a loss in the long run,

or

(5) It's no good to waste your emotional energy on it, since people have always done wrong and always will,

or

(6) No matter how big a deal it seems to you now, it has no cosmic significance whatsoever, so maybe you should just get over it.

Marcus is a writer who must take an exalted place of pride in the "It's really no big deal" literature of consolation and level-headedness. A sample nugget will illustrate his attitude:

> All things quickly pass away and become no more than a story, and complete oblivion soon buries them. (IV.33)

Don't you wish that he had added, "But have a nice day anyway"?

The point here, of course, is to help us control our almost instinctively negative responses to any particular unwanted event, not allowing our emotional reactions to unhinge us and lead us into inconsistent behavior. All the Stoic philosophers were acutely aware of the role our passions can play in messing up our lives, and they wanted to help us stay in control. Sometimes, as a result, as we have seen earlier, these otherwise practical thinkers failed to appreciate the potential importance of positive emotion, or passion put to the service of our goals. But, as we also have noted, we can derive great practical wisdom from good philosophers who are far from being perfectly balanced and completely correct in their own views. It's up to us to find what is most insightful in their advice, and put that wisdom to work with balance and perspective in our lives. Although Marcus shares the usual Stoic uneasiness about the emotional side of life, we can benefit from looking briefly at what he does have to say about emotion in a positive vein.

22

POSITIVE EMOTION

The positive role of emotion, or the role of the positive emotions, in a successful journey through life is relatively neglected in Marcus Aurelius's writings, and is generally underappreciated in the overall Stoic philosophy of life, as we have had occasion to note. And so we won't find the Emperor encouraging us to find something in life that we are passionate about, to follow our loves, to be as enthusiastic as we can, or to use the power of our imaginations to build an emotional commitment to the importance of what we are doing, day to day. Like Seneca and Epictetus, he is so concerned about the destructive impact of negative emotion in human life that he seems largely unable to acknowledge the wonderful effect that positive emotion can have.

Not every great thinker or wise advisor in human history has seen or discussed the importance of everything that other observant philosophers may have discerned. Even the most perceptive people can indeed sometimes have prejudices or blind spots, habits of thought or feeling that block insight into some facet of life. But our Stoic general, for all his silence on the positive motivational role of emotion in our own lives, does say some very interesting things that are relevant to the topic when he addresses the subject of working with other people. First, consider a somewhat enigmatic passage where he exhorts us:

> Whenever you notice anyone doing anything, make it a habit to ask yourself, "Why is he really doing this?" But first ask this same question of your own actions.
>
> Remember that what pulls the strings of our lives is always deep inside, and often hidden from view. It

> is the power of persuasion. It is the source of life. It
> is the essence of a man. (X.37–38)

And then:

> Pay attention to the ruling principles that incline
> people to act as they do. Examine especially the
> wise. Notice what they avoid, and what they pursue.
> (IV.38)

It may be a little bit of a stretch for me to read him this way, but Marcus seems here to be acknowledging that it is the inner life of attraction and repulsion, or precisely the life of the emotions and attitudes, that is the ultimate wellspring of motivation and action. Even here, however, he tries to rationalize it by referring to "principles," as if all motivation is a matter of following explicit rules or generalizations. But what is the relation between a principle and a person? The person must be attracted to the principle, or to the thing that the principle endorses, in order to be motivated to apply that principle in action. This sort of relation of attraction is precisely a kind of emotional commitment.

So the emotions after all cannot be completely expunged from the realm of motivation by any realistic philosophy of life that embraces positive achievement. The emotions are at the core of human motivation. In fact, even more strongly, motivation is all about emotional commitment, an emotional tie to whatever it is that we value.

The Stoics recognized that we are often derailed from our paths by negative emotion, and sometimes even by positive feelings. Marcus, like Epictetus and other Stoics, realized that anger, frustration, despair, or a sense of desperation, can certainly cause us to act in ways that are self-defeating. But they also were aware that intensely positive emotions can have the same result. Exhilaration, infatuation, or a sense of thrill, can cause you to do things that you would never contemplate "if you were in your right mind," as we say. So, as we have seen, the Stoics wanted to help free us from the bondage of overwrought emotions of any kind. Emotion is intrinsically so powerful, they seemed to think, that we are best off keeping our distance. But the same wave that can knock you off your feet can be surfed by someone going in the right direction, with the right equipment, the right skill, and the right balance.

Anything with great potential for ill has correspondingly great potential for good, or else arises out of something with that potential. If emotion can destroy a person, it can also, properly directed, bring a person the power, the initiative, and the persistence to attain great and positive success. It is a power within, Marcus acknowledges, a hidden persuader inside us that really gives life. And this hidden persuader is nothing other than the power of emotional commitment, without which we can never fully flourish as we are capable of flourishing.

Perhaps, in the end, even a Stoic thinker like Marcus, who is leery of disturbing emotions, could admit to this. The emotional commitment that moves positive conduct is different in nature from the sudden, tumultuous, transient emotional feelings that all the Stoics were so careful to guard against. It is more like a lively belief or an enhanced affirmation. It is positive energy in service to perceived good. And what could be bad about that?

23

THE DEMANDS OF
INTEGRITY

The ancient philosophers most often saw deeply enough into the nature of successful living to recognize the unparalleled importance of good character in everything we do. Moral goodness, or integrity of character, doesn't necessarily guarantee the attainment of any particular external results in any specific situation, but it does facilitate the impact that ultimately we are here to have on the world.

There are people who at some level feel the tug of goodness on their innermost being, but are prepared to put off its demands for the sake of the temporary appearance of immediate gain. "There's always time for nobility," they rationalize somewhere within their innermost souls, "but I've got to take advantage of this opportunity as it presents itself now," which often translates as "I've got to take advantage of this person or I won't get what I want."

We often find in life that it seems easy to put off the truly important while the screaming demands of apparent urgency bully us along. It can be especially difficult to walk the straight and narrow when everyone around us seems to be dancing to the tunes of easy expediency. Marcus, in his inimitable way, is blunt. He teaches us:

> Don't act as if you were going to live a thousand years. Death hangs over you now. While you are alive, while it is in your power, be good. (IV.17)

Other things can wait. Goodness can't. Marcus then follows this by the note:

> A man saves himself a lot of trouble when he doesn't look to see what his neighbor says or does or thinks, but only considers whether his own

> actions are just and pure. As Agathon recommends,
> don't be distracted by the corrupt morals of others,
> but run straight toward your proper goal without
> deviating from it. (IV.18)

Each of us should have an inner compass to steer by. We need
our own sense of what is right, and should not let ourselves be dis-
tracted from that by the potentially different conduct displayed by
any of the people around us. Marcus believes that if we have the
right values and are true to ourselves, we will put ourselves in the
best possible position to make the decisions we need to make. In
everything we do, we should walk straight, and that requires both
cultivating strength within and protecting ourselves from the potentially corrupting influence of anyone around us who is not equally
committed to the life of integrity.

We should ourselves be good and ethical in all we do. But in
addition, it's also a good idea to do everything in our power not to
work with, depend on, or even associate with other people who are
not likewise prepared to follow the demands of goodness. One of
my old friends likes to say, "You can't make a good deal with a bad
man". No matter how good a deal of any kind sounds, if it's with a
bad person, you can be assured that it will end up being bad for you.

In one passage, Marcus describes the unethical person as
"tearing his own face", destroying and condemning himself by his
selfishly calculated actions that fall outside the bounds of the
morally acceptable. Unethical conduct is always, in the end, self-
destructive. By deviating from what is good and right, we undermine our own projects and prospects in this world. But it's also
important to understand that by working with, or linking ourselves to, people with bad character, we also set ourselves up for
serious problems.

To think you can associate or work well with a bad man and
constrain the harm of his mischief is folly. Our philosopher says:

> You should realize that expecting a bad man
> not to do wrong is like expecting fig trees not to
> grow juicy fruit, babies not to cry, and horses not
> to neigh. It's like expecting the inevitable not to
> happen. (XII.16)

He immediately follows this by writing:

If it's not right, don't do it; if it's not true, don't say
it. (XII.17)

It's tempting to some people, especially in their business lives,
to think it's all right to have as an associate a human pit bull, a person capable of lashing out mercilessly at anyone outside the company, or the office, who gets in the way, and prepared to do almost
anything to anyone on the outside just to get the results that are
wanted by those on the inside. But Marcus points out again that:

> To expect bad men not to do wrong is crazy.
> Anyone who thinks this way wants the impossible.
> But to allow them to treat other people badly, and
> then expect them not to do the same to you, is both
> irrational and arrogant. (XI.18)

We should expect the highest conduct from the people we work
with, if what we are concerned about is true and noble success,
long term and deeply satisfying achievement of which we can be
proud. And this is tied to expecting the best from ourselves. We
should never preach to our associates what we don't practice in our
own daily conduct. Marcus says:

> You can't teach other people the rules of reading
> and writing before you have first learned to follow
> them yourself. The same is true of life. (XI.29)

No one wants to listen to a hypocrite. A drowning man has trouble teaching others to swim.

So how can we see to it that in our own behavior we always
take the high road? Marcus joins his fellow Stoic thinkers in holding that we need not just rules and an inner determination to follow those rules, but an imaginatively powerful model for ethical
success. The Emperor puts it this way:

> In the writings of the Ephesians, there was this
> suggestion: Keep in your mind at all times the image
> of some virtuous person from the past. (XI.26)

It turns out that this is not only one of the most ancient, but also
one of the most potent, pieces of ethical advice ever given. One

contemporary company president has told me he suggests to every one of his colleagues that we all need to carry around in our heads the image of one or two people, historical figures of powerful character or personal mentors that we admire, and that we should be prepared to ask ourselves, in any moral or ethical situation, what that person would do if faced with the same choices. From the prehistoric human past, we are deep down emulators, imprinting from those we look to, and, because of this, we should look only to those we most admire. Marcus and the other Stoics share this recommendation with men and women of insight throughout the ages. It is good and powerful advice indeed.

Our philosopher understands that the royal road to lasting success lies along the moral high ground. Goodness is so important that there is a real urgency to moral living. Any day that we deviate from the straight ethical path that our hearts deeply recognize is a day we tear our own faces, severely disfiguring our appearance to those around us, and undermining the long term effects for good that we otherwise could have. As Marcus realized, all the wealth of an empire, fame throughout the world, and unparalleled worldly power cannot add up to the great value and lasting importance of a fully good life.

This is a message from millennia past that so many of us have to learn again the hard way. But, however we come to it, it is worth the trouble, and can change our lives dramatically. The demands of integrity are the doorway to inner peace, deep fulfillment, and the only sort of achievement that can last.

24

LIVING AT PEACE

We don't have a lot of advice from Marcus Aurelius that is directly on the issue of enjoying life, because of the general Stoic reticence about positive emotions that we have already noted several times. But we do see something interesting in this regard throughout his meditations. Many of the distinctive thought experiments of Stoicism that are engaged in by Marcus and other philosophers—for example, those that involve remembering the transitory nature of life, the ever present possibility of death, and our smallness in the universe—are, somewhat ironically on first glance, all techniques meant to help us keep things from preventing our peaceful enjoyment of our ongoing daily experience.

The Stoics are always counseling us to cool down, take it easy, and not let things get under our skin. They want to help rid us of anything that would trouble or disturb us. And, of course, this means that they prescribe attitudes and mental reminders that, when properly used, can free up our enjoyment of the process of daily living and working, however difficult it might otherwise sometimes seem.

I have to admit that I tend to take a celebratory approach to life, as much as any particular day allows me to do so. I usually view most of life as a festival, occasionally as a carnival, sometimes as a party, and even occasionally as a dance. Marcus viewed it very differently, as in many ways a contest. He declares, in an apt choice of simile:

> The art of living is more like wrestling than
> dancing in one respect: you have to stay on your
> feet steady and ready to meet any blows that are
> sudden and unexpected. (VII.61)

All the Stoics were concerned to help us deal with the some-times unpleasant surprises that life can send our way. They did not want us to become unhinged. They hoped to prepare us to such an extent that neither dread, nor anxiety, nor shock would ever keep us from experiencing a sense of inner resilience and inner peace as we move through this world.

Marcus himself wanted to be able to face anything in this world with equanimity. But in one place even he goes so far as to say that he wants to be able to face the world with "delight." This is not a term that most people expect a Stoic to use. He remarks:

Different things delight different people. My delight is in keeping my mind clear and untroubled without ignoring any man or anything that happens to men, while dealing with everyone compassionate-ly, and using everything according to its real value. (VIII.43)

The philosopher will never shield his eyes from the troubles of the world, but in full sight of whatever this life has to offer, he will find his own personal delight in the proper ordering of the only things truly within his control—his inner attitudes and will. And this, he thinks, is enough.

Marcus Aurelius advises us:

Always keep this in mind: that very little is necessary for living a happy life. (VII.67)

Marcus brings a laser-like focus to his advice, and in one passage maintains that:

If you will concentrate on living what is really your life—the present moment —then you will be able to live the rest of your life free from anxiety, nobly, and at peace with your own spirit—with the god that is within you. (XII.3)

His message is simple. Embrace the present fully. This is where your real life is, and that is where peace and delight are to be found. This will also put you most fully in touch with "the god that is within you," that spark of the spirit most likely to lead you into your own deepest personal fulfillment.

Yes, free yourself from negative perturbations, but also have a little fun. Savor the journey of your life as you live it.

The ancients often said, "Know thyself." Using, but going a step beyond anything that our three Stoic guides might ever explicitly recommend, I want to add, "Enjoy thyself!"—and I'd even like to tack on, "Now!" I have come to believe that this is just as important as anything else we can do, in its power to help us position ourselves to be who we most deeply are, and to make our mark, long term, in this life.

The Stoics give us some very good advice. They offer many powerful suggestions to help us build up those inner foundations we all need for living a life of resilience, strength, and positive achievement. But, sometimes, taking it all to heart, we still have to add a good measure of our own insight into the mix.

Life is a performance art. Proper achievement is a performance art. We are all meant to be artists, learning and creating as we go. The distinctive perspectives of the three great Stoic thinkers can help us on our way as we seek to make our difference in this world, enjoy our proper forms of success, and experience that inner happiness that otherwise might have seemed so elusive. With a little ancient wisdom to build on, we can move forward more strongly, more effectively, and more confidently into the future. Why indeed should we ever settle for anything less?

INDEX